CELEBRATING FRIENDS AND FRIENDSHIP

Praise for *Celebrating Friends and Friendship* by Dr. Jan Yager

"Friendships are priceless. Dr. Jan Yager's new book, *Celebrating Friends and Friendships*, is also priceless. Totally worth reading."
—Jeffrey J. Fox, author, *How to Become a Rainmaker*

"I am grateful for my friendships and grateful that Jan Yager has written a book that helps me to celebrate my friendships and their power every day!"
—Leslie A. Yerkes, author, *301 Ways to Have Fun at Work*

"As someone who values my friends, I'm always looking for additional ideas about how to let them know I care. That's why I really appreciate Jan Yager's book, *Celebrating Friends and Friendship*. It's a fun book with lots of practical information as well as provocative sociological insights into friendship, gift-giving, and even the value of rituals."
—Dara Tyson, freelance publicist

"As a person whose circle of friends has gradually been reduced, whether through pandemic proximities, attrition, or sheer neglect, Jan's book, *Celebrating Friends and Friendship,* has rejuvenated my awareness of how important and fulfilling my friendships have been, and still can be, in enriching my life."
—Bob McGee, author, *A View Through the Fog*

Selected Books by Jan Yager

CELEBRATING FRIENDS & FRIENDSHIP

Hannacroix Creek Books, Inc.
Stamford, Connecticut

This book is dedicated to all my wonderful friends —current, past, and future. Thank you for being there for me. You enrich my life, and I hope you realize how much I like and love all of you.

Thanks also to my husband Fred and our family. You mean the world to me.

The picture on the half-title page is courtesy of Shutterstock, photo contributor: Jacob Lund. The photograph on the title page is courtesy of Shutterstock, contributor is Nuvi Frames. The flower at the end of the Contents page is by Dr. Jan Yager.

Published by:
Hannacroix Creek Books, Inc.
1127 High Ridge Road, #110
Stamford, CT 06905 USA
e-mail: hannacroix@aol.com
https://www.hannacroixcreekbooks.com

Disclaimer
This publication contains the opinions and ideas of its author and is designed to provide useful information regarding the subject matter covered. It is sold with the understanding that the author and publisher are not engaged in rendering legal, psychological, or professional services in this publication. Inclusion of products, services, associations, or companies does not imply an endorsement. Websites, e-m ails, and other information can change in an instant. It is the reader's responsibility to apply due diligence regarding any general information in this book.

ISBN: 978-1-938998-63-8 (paperback)
ISBN: 978-1-938998-64-5 (hardcover)

Also available as an e-book

Library of Congress Control Number: 2024904359

Contents

Introduction

Courtesy of Shutterstock. Contributor: Rawpixel.com

Why Remember and Celebrate Our Friends

Over the decades of my friendship research, there are statements that I hear repeatedly. One of them is, "I'd get together with my friends if I just had more time." Another is how easy it is to stay connected because of social media, but how many of you now feel like you don't have those one or two intimate friendships anymore because social media has replaced real connecting.

The question becomes whether those friendships were ever that close to begin with, or if social media and being busy has really been a factor in why a friendship drifts apart.

There are also factors that life inevitably hands us: friendships that end because of a friend's passing because of illness or even sudden death. The number of articles, blogs, and social media posts when Matthew Perry, one of the original cast members of the hit TV show *Friends*, died on October 28th, 2023, allegedly from drowning in his hot tub, were filled with shock and sadness. That's how I felt when my close friend Sharon died suddenly two years ago from illness. Our friendship spanned four decades. Or when I did a Google search to see if my close friend Elia, a filmmaker and acting teacher who relocated from Venezuela and New York to California, was at a film festival or involved in a project in another country as the reason she wasn't returning my phone call or my e-mails. Unfortunately, I was shocked to find her obituary announcing that she had died from a rare cancer.

1

Florida-based Suellyn Bache shared with me about her best friend of more than 40 years. In her reflections, we are reminded of how key it is to remember to celebrate our friends:

> We met in a supermarket in Stamford [Connecticut] while waiting in line at the deli counter. She approached me and we exchanged phone numbers. There ensued a 40+ year friendship, full of laughs, adventures, traveling together, shopping, telling each other our deepest, darkest secrets, and helping each other when needed. She helped me tremendously when I suffered a year long illness. We were so simpatico! We eventually moved into the same community in Florida, which was wonderful.
>
> Unfortunately, she is now in the deep throws of dementia, completely bedridden, and mostly non-verbal. I do see her from time-to-time and love her so much. She would hate what she looks like [now] but is very well taken care of by round-the-clock aides. It is so, so sad for me to lose her this way.

Suellyn's example reminds us that whatever our age, we need to enjoy our friends and to celebrate each other. We all need to let our friends know through words and deeds that they matter to us and that is why I decided to write this book. I conceived of it as a way of facilitating that outpouring of appreciation for our friends and for friendship, through words and deeds.

Trona T.K. Peoples

Trona "T.K." Peoples, an educator and school librarian in Georgia, put it quite eloquently:

> Friendship is a beautiful and vital aspect of our lives. We are all mothers, wives, girlfriends, working women, and so much more. We need that source of joy and support that only friends can give sometimes. This is why celebrating each other is necessary. My friends and I live by the fact that we know tomorrow isn't always promised. So, we take every opportunity to love and celebrate each other.
>
> Celebrating friends is a two-way street. It's not just about one-sided appreciation, but a mutual exchange of affection and gratitude. I am such a giver than I often tell my friends they do not have to celebrate me. But when they do, I am overjoyed and feel so loved. I treasure the time, thought, and energy they used to celebrate and honor me. It reinforces that I am important in their lives.

Dr. HermanSJr., a Global Change Agent, shares why he sees celebrating our friends as such an essential thing to do, as well as some of the ways to do it:

> Celebrating friendships makes all parties feel accepted and positive. Such [celebrating] also empowers these parties to advance in, or past, whatever they wish (e.g., advance in academic and business goals, or advance past sadness and loneliness). True friendship is a symbiont circle.

Celebrating friendships is a must, just as doing so for any system is. By "celebration" I meant it per etymology – practice regularly for solemnity. Ergo, the celebration need not be a party or big gathering. It can even be an often (although not necessarily regularly scheduled) hangout with just two (or more) people. That includes getting one macchiato at a café, a beer at a bar, a pizza slice at a pizzeria, playing a round of golf, bowling, or darts, meditating at a temple, or even sitting on the porch steps of one of your houses while people watching.

Why This Book

I had just finished the workbook, *Putting WHEN FRIENDSHIP HURTS to Work: Exercises and Activities to Deal with Friends Who Betray, Abandon, or Wound You, Plus Help in Finding and Keeping Good Friends*. The workbook is a companion guide to *When Friendship Hurts,* but goes beyond dealing with challenging friendships, although that is its focus and the vital issue addressed in *When Friendship Hurts.*

It occurred to me that what I should do now is create a book that focused on the joys of friendship. The result is *Celebrating Friends & Friendship.* I also wanted to write a book illustrated with color photographs, as well as original artwork showing friendship in action. I envisioned the book where you could not only learn about celebrating friendship, but where you could even plan, or record, how you and your friends celebrate each other, whether those celebrations are material, non-material, or experiential.

If you've read some of my books on friendship, you may already know scientific research confirms that having even one friend can extend your life. There are the physical benefits of having a friend including everything from delaying or possibly even stopping the onset of dementia to being able to recover faster from illnesses, including a heart attack and cancer.

But there are also the emotional benefits of having a friend to talk to and to get support from when things are tough in your life, and even when things go well, and you want someone besides a romantic partner or other family members to share it with. Some of us are lucky enough to have a loving spouse and children and even grandchildren, but others are single either by choice or circumstances, and they may also not have children, or their children may live far away. So, for them, friends are the key relationships in their lives.

Another reason I was motivated to write this book is that I learned a lot about the importance of celebrations and rituals when I taught "Sociology of Culture" at Iona University in the Fall 2023. Our main textbook was *An Introduction to Popular Culture on the US: People, Politics, and Power*, by co-authors Jenn Brandt, associate professor of Women's Studies at California State University, and Callie Clare, assistant professor of Communications at Siena Heights University.

In their chapter on "Rituals and Ceremonies," Brandt and Clare emphasize that celebrations are applied to "something that stands outside of the ordinary in a positive way." (Brandt and Clare, page 225) as the co-authors note, it is that the celebrations "stand apart from the activities of daily life" that makes them so powerful.

One of the ways these celebrations take on a specific meaning, and duplication, is through rituals. How important are rituals? In my October-November 2023 snowball sample of 37 men and women in the U.S. and in several countries about what friendship-related rituals they participated in, a female respondent in her 70s wrote, "The rituals are like glue. If there is no glue, it's harder to stay together." In that survey, the two most popular friendship rituals were "getting together for a birthday celebration" (81%) followed by "sending a birthday card" (70%). Also, birthday-related was the third most popular friendship ritual, sending a birthday present (57%), which was tied with "participating in a regular activity together."

The next most popular ritual, almost as popular as the previous one, was "going on a friend getaway weekend (51%) with the popularity of the next rituals dropping quite a bit: going on a friend getaway longer vacation (32%); with the next rituals tied between "having parties besides birthday parties" (27%) or volunteering together (27%).

It was surprising that "playing sports together" was a ritual cited only by 13% of this population of men and women between the ages of 18 and 79.

Most of us associate rituals with the religion we grew up in and, if you choose to, you perpetuate in your adult years and in how you parent your children. Rituals can be applied to our friendships as well, although it always needs to be optional and voluntary. There are already too many "shoulds" in our lives. We don't need to add a "friendship should" to the mix. Besides, it could turn a positive, fun celebration or ritual into a mandatory requirement that soon backfires by potentially creating distance rather than intimacy.

Chapter 1

Friendship and Gift Giving: An Overview

This photo by unknown author is licensed under CC BY-SA. Courtesy of Microsoft Word.

The Value of Friendship

Hopefully we are all fortunate to have at least one friend we can laugh with and have some fun. Stan Holden, author of *Growing Your Business Can be as Fun & Easy as... Giving Candy to Strangers*, says, "I have a lot of friends, male and female. My very close friends are guys I have known since high school. We're warriors together, having each other's back."

It is vital to also mention the physical and mental benefits of positive friendships that go far beyond that "feeling good" state. As I point out in *Friendgevity,* quoting Lynne C. Giles, e. al., in her study, *Effect of Social Networks on 10-year Survival in Very Old Australian*s, "It is friends, rather than children or relatives, which confer [the] most benefit to survival in later life." (Giles, et. al., 2005)

Here are some other studies that emphasize the value friends have in our lives:

- Studies by Hartup and Colarossi and Eccles have found that adolescents with friends have greater self-esteem and are "happier on average." (Cited by Manchanda, Stein and Fazel, January 25, 2023)
- According to academics at University College London, someone who saw a friend daily at the age of 60 was 12% less likely to get dementia than someone who only saw one or two friends every couple of months. (Tom Horton, August 3, 2019)
- In researching *Growing Young: How Friendship, Optimism, and Kindness Can Help You Live to 100*, Marta Zaraska discovered that volunteering lowers your mortality risk by 22%. (Zaraska, *Growing Young*)

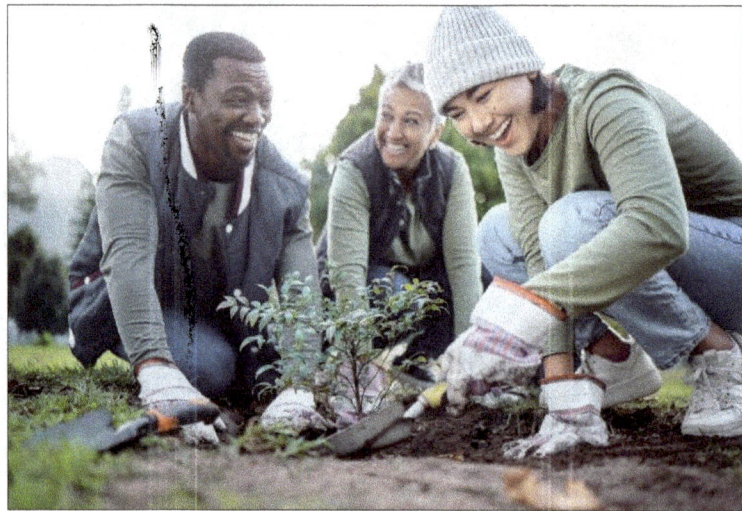

Courtesy of Shutterstock. Contributor: PeopleImages.com - Yuri A.

- Loneliness is now considered a health crisis considered a much as a potential health concern as smoking as many as 15 cigarettes a day. (Mikhail, Forbes, June 15, 2023)

Courtesy of Shutterstock. Contributor - Chutharat Kamkhuntee

6

Dealing with Loneliness

Loneliness is something sociologists and psychologists have been studying and writing about for decades. But it has become more of an epidemic of late. A national survey conducted in October 2020 by Harvard University's Graduate School of Education's Making Caring Common Project of 950 American men and women found that overall, 36% of those in the study reported feeling lonely "frequently" or "almost all the time or all the time" in the previous four weeks. Another 36% reported being occasionally lonely. Those with the highest percentage of loneliness were young adults between the ages of 18-25- 61% described themselves as seriously lonely. The second group were the mothers with young children; 51% described themselves as seriously lonely. Although the report on the study does not include statistics, it does "suggest other population that may be prone to loneliness, including single (never married), divorced, and separated adults…" (Weissbound, et. al., page 8)

Since this study was conducted during the height of the COVID pandemic, when many states had mandatory lockdowns, that is a factor that must be taken into a count. But more recent studies and reports are highlighting that loneliness is still a major issue in the U.S. A May 3, 2023 press release entitled, "New Surgeon General Advisory Raises Alarm about the Devastating Impact of the Epidemic of Loneliness and Isolation in the United States" discusses United States Surgeon General Dr. Vivek Murthy's concern about loneliness that he indicated pre-dated the pandemic. The press release states: "The physical health consequences of poor or insufficient connection include a 29% increased risk of heart disease, a 32% increased risk of stroke, and a 50% increased risk of developing dementia for older adults. Furthermore, lacking social connection increases risk of premature death by more than 60%."

What are the causes of loneliness? In sociology we point to the work of C. Wright Mills dating back to the 1950s and his concept of a personal trouble versus a social issue. There are individuals for whom loneliness is an outgrowth of their own personalities which might include shyness or failing to get the bonding with one or both parents or caregivers during the formative years that makes it hard for those individuals to reach out to others.

But when loneliness reaches the epidemic proportions as it has in the United States, we would call this a social issue. What are the contributing factors? Exclusive remote work is a factor. Working remotely one or two days a week could be a welcome change of pace for those with long commutes but five days a week, especially for those who are single and living alone, could be contributing to their loneliness,

Too much social media isn't good for you. Katherine Hobson in her article, "Feeling Lonely? Too Much Time on Social Media May Be Why" posted at NPR.com pointed out that reported on a study in the American Journal of Preventive Medicine by Primack, M.D., et. al. that discovered that "the people who reported spending the most time on social media — more than two hours a day — had twice the odds of perceived social isolation than those who said they spent a half hour per day or less on those sites." (Hobson, NPR.com)

Used wisely and appropriately, social media can be a boost to connectiveness but only if it is just one of many ways of communicating with friends. If it becomes the sole way of interacting, with phone calls or in-person meetings no longer taking place, loneliness is more likely to occur.

As indicated at the very beginning of the Introduction to this book, the "I'm busy" excuse for failing to get together with friends is a key factor. Unfortunately, if you are too busy too often those friends are going to turn their attention to others who will make the time for them. It can take months or even as long as three years to develop a tried-and-true friendship; it can end in an instant so celebrating your friends that you want to keep in your life is one way to avoid the loneliness that too many are experiencing today.

There are also too many articles emphasizing that getting over a friendship breakup can be harder than getting over the end of a romance or marriage. There may be some that find that to be the case, but in my experience breaking up with a friend, although it's unpleasant and stressful, does not dramatically change the course of someone's life the way a romantic breakup does especially if the couple were married, living together, and shared children not to mention a bank account.

The point is that if someone has intimacy fears, emphasizing that friendship breakups are so traumatic could instil enough fear in someone to push them away from seeking out and cultivating friendships, especially close or best friendships.

There's an adage, "Tis better to have loved and lost than never to have never loved at all" and most of us probably think that relates to romantic love. But the phrase, attributed to British poet Alred Tennyson (1809-1892) was published in 1850 as part of his elegy to his closest friend Arthur Henry Hallum, who died suddenly at the age of 22 in 1833. (Bex Roden, August 24, 2023)

The good news is that positive friendships can assuage loneliness.

What Most of Us Want in a Friend

Here's the acronym I created related to the word *friendshifts* and my related book, *Friendshifts*:

F = Friendly
R = Reliable
I – Interests are shared and/or appreciated.
E – Empathy
N = Not related by blood or marriage
D = Discretion; dealing with any conflicts
S = Shared values
H = Honesty
I = Intimacy (as much as is acceptable)
F = Faithful; neither fair nor foul
T = Trust

S – Support each other emotionally

What Are the Responsibilities of Being a Friend?

Here is another way of thinking about what we want in a friend, as well as what we need to consider about our own behavior when it comes to friendship, by taking the Friendship Oath. As I wrote in my workbook, *Putting WHEN FRIENDSHIP HURTS to Work,* "The Friendship Oath is something I developed when I realized that we have an oath for marriage. Why not an oath for friendship?" Here's a reprint of that oath:

The Friendship Oath

By accepting the responsibility of friendship, I promise to be honest and trustworthy. I will try to work out any conflicts that we may have and will try to put the time and effort into our friendship that it requires.

I know we both have work (or school), family, and personal obligations, and we will respect each other's other relationships and commitments, but I will also be committed to this friendship. I will try to only give advice if you ask for it, unless, in my best judgment, I volunteer it. I will also try to always be your friend, unconditionally.

I will keep your confidences. However, I will also share with you if it is my policy to never keep anything from my spouse or any other primary relationship, with whom I entrust all my secrets.

I will try to remember your birthday and be there for you when times are tough, and when times are grand.

Making time to talk by phone, communicating by mail, e-mail, or text, or getting together in person is a priority. I will celebrate your achievements even though I know a tiny bit of envy or competitiveness is normal.

I will bring fun and joy to your life as much as I am able to as I cherish our past, present, and future friendship.

Twenty Friendship Affirmations

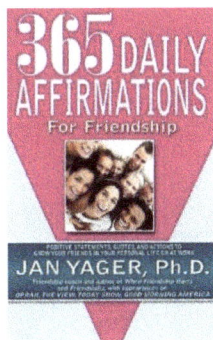

It is challenging to pick 20 friendship affirmations out of 365, but here are my choices. Besides, this gave me an opportunity to reread all the affirmations in my book, *365 Daily Affirmations for Friendship* (Hannacroix Creek Books, Inc., 2012). Please consider writing your own friendship affirmations as well! As you probably know, affirmations are written in the present and not as "I will" statements about the future.

The numbers in front of the affirmations that follow correspond to where the affirmation appears in the original book.

1. *I am worthy of a positive friendship.*
2. *I like and love myself.*
3. *Physical distance is much easier to overcome between true friends than emotional distance.*
4. *I put the time and energy into friendship that any worthwhile intimate relationship requires.*
7. *I am realistic in my demands on*

my friends.

16. *I am loyal and devoted.*

26. *I remember my friends' birthdays in whatever way I can, but it is the concern that counts.*

54. *Keeping promises I make to my friends is the cornerstone of a reliable friend.*

57. *If a friendship is worth saving, I work hard to deal with any conflicts with my friend rather than end our relationship.*

85. *I avoid asking my friends to choose between our friendship and their romantic or parenting relationships.*

121. *I am a good listener, striving to be an even better one.*

173. *when my friends achieve, I achieve.*

249. *I am open and honest while still being tactful.*

266. *"How are you?" are three little words that have so much meaning when asked of a friend.*

299. *I am careful not to betray my friends.*

300. *I forgive myself for ending a friendship.*

301. *I forgive any friends who end our friendship.*

310. *I remember my friends all year round.*

332. *I study friendship and how to be a better friend.*

365. *I embrace travel as an opportunity to reconnect with old friends and to meet new ones.*

Ten Selected Famous Friendship Quotes

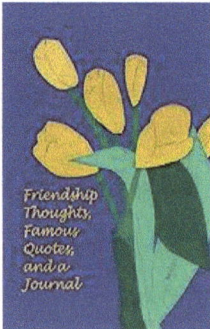

There are more than 100 famous friendship quotes in the journal, *Friendship Thoughts, Famous Quotes, and a Journal* (Hannacroix Creek Books, 2014). Like the challenge of choosing 20 friendship affirmations out of 365, it is quite the task to choose my 10 preferred famous friendship quotes. In making those choices, I tried to select quotes from ancient times through to more contemporary eras. Here are my top 10:

"We can learn to be our own best friend. If we do, we have a friend for life."
—Mildred Newman and Bernard Berkowitz, with Jean Owen, *How to Be Your Own Best Friend* (1971).

"Friendship consists in forgetting what one gives and remembering what one receives."
—Alexandre Dumas, French writer (1802-1870)

"In research at our clinic, my colleagues and I have discovered that friendship is the springboard to the other important relationships of life." —psychotherapist Alan Loy McGinnis, *The Friendship Factor* (1979)

"A friend may well be reckoned the masterpiece of nature." —Ralph Waldo Emerson (1803-1882), "Friendship" Essays (1841)

"If you want to win friends, make a point to remember them. If you remember my name, you pay me a subtle compliment. You indicate that I have made an impression on you. Remember my name and you add to my feeling of importance."

—Dale Carnegie, *How to Win Friends and Influence People* (1936)

"What is a friend? A single soul dwelling in two bodies." —Aristotle (384-322 B.C.)

"A Father's a Treasure; a Brother's a Comfort; a Friend is Both." — Benjamin Franklin, *Poor Richard's Almanac* (1732)

"I rejoice in others' successes, knowing that there is plenty for us all."— Louise L. Hay, #45, *Power Thoughts: 365 Daily Affirmations* (1999)

"No receipt openeth the heart, but a true friend to whom you may impart griefs, joys, fears, hopes, suspicions, counsels, and whatsoever lieth upon the heart to oppress it, in a kind of civil shrift or confession."—Sir Francis Bacon, "Of Friendship" (1625)

"It is hard to say, 'I need friends.'"
—Shasta Nelson, *Friendships Don't Just Happen* (2013)

15 Key Friendship Insights

If you have read one or more of my books on friendship you may find many of these ideas familiar to you. But if you haven't, certain ideas about friendship may be news to you. Either way, I hope you find this knowledge about friendship to be informative and useful whether it is a review or new.

1. In ancient times, when marriage tended to be based on convenience more than romantic love, having what I refer to as a "great friend" was a relationship that was exalted. Consider how many of the philosophers have written about friendship: Cicero, Aristotle, Plato. Beginning with the introduction of romantic love, and the idea that a romantic partner could also be a companion, we see the development of what I call the "Contemporary Friend." For those who are married or have a strong romantic bond with another, it is harder for friends to be as intimate as they once were since the romantic partner is, ideally, also a friend. So, friendship and marriage must co-exist, one of the major *friendshifts* in life. It is up to each romantic couple to find a way that is a possibility.
2. Shared values are the best predictor of longevity in a friendship.
3. The average number of friends I discovered are 1-2 best friends, 4-6 close friends, and 10-25 casual friends but this number varies by an individual's subjective definitions of each kind of friend. Social media has also dramatically increased the number of casual friends for many to 50, 100, or even more.
4. Social media can help friends to communicate more quickly and regularly but be careful to share the big news with your close or best friends first *before* anything is posted online.
5. Honesty is the best policy with friendship, but you still must be tactful and to be careful that honesty does not border on cruelty or even rudeness. Although if there is a life-threatening situation, such as suspicions of abuse, being honest so a friend gets the help she/he needs is what friends do.

6. Beware of the "I am busy" syndrome. It can be an understandable situation that needs to be understood, or it could be covering up an avoidance of a friend because there are issues that need to be resolved.
7. The wish to have a lifelong ideal friendship has for some replaced the goal of having a lifelong marriage and not just a marriage but a "perfect" union.
8. Keeping a friendship going takes work, but it is not the same as working at a job because you need the money. Working on being a better friend may mean trying to put in the time and effort to be a better listener, or to get together in person, because you value your friend.
9. The sociologist George Simmel looked at the characteristics of small group dynamics. Dyads are more intimate, but the two-person connection is more unstable and ends if one person dissolves it. Triads can last longer because one person withdrawing does not end the group. But there is no such thing as a friendship of three equals. It is always two plus one with the alliance's possibility shifting all the time.
10. The power of friendship is in its voluntary status. That means it must be freely given and it needs to be mutual or reciprocal. With that power comes the risk that it could be ended at any moment, especially if it is a dyad or a two-person friendship.
11. As I wrote in my book *Friendshifts*, who our friends are may change or shift over time and even how we define a friend, and that is okay.
12. Probably one of the hardest lessons for all of us to learn, and one that I write about in *When Friendship Hurts* and *Putting WHEN FRIENDSHIP HURTS to Work,* is that letting go of any angst or regrets and appreciating however long that friendship lasted is a gift we all should give ourselves.
13. New friends are always available. Whatever your age, marital status, gender, religion, race, or ethnicity, there is a potential friend that you just must meet. The quoteinvestigator.com attributes the statement "That strangers are friends that we may someday meet." to the 1915 poem "Faith" by Edgar Guest, rather than to Irish poet Wiliam Butler Yeats (August 9, 2017).
14. Since friends are not connected by blood, legal contracts, or, in most cases, sex, ideally it should be easier to find and cultivate a new friendship than finding a romantic partner with whom one enters a more complex and intimate relationships which may include financial, legal, and even parental responsibilities.
15. Finally, you can't force someone to like you, but you can certainly work harder at making yourself likeable even if there are no guarantees that it will positively impact a conflictual friendship.

Gift Giving as Exchange

This book looks at celebrating our friends including gift-giving; gift-giving need not be material. It could be emotional or experiential and the experience could be just hanging out together. What is not stressed often enough, especially for those who are beyond adolescence with lots of school, work, or family obligations, is the "fun factor" in friendship and celebrating our friends. Hopefully you can have fun with your romantic partner and with your children, but since friendship is voluntary and a relationship outside of our everyday familial, work, school, or even community obligations, connecting with our friends can inject fun beyond all the "have to dos" that we all need to deal with.

There is some truth to the updated saying "all work and no play make (pick a name) a dull person." We need to have fun. We need to play. There's an organization, the Red Hat Society – an association for women over 50 who just get together to have fun and friendship. It was founded more than 20 years ago and now has a worldwide membership of an estimated 1.5 million members and over 40,000 chapters.

Having fun with a friend is a gift. And it can't be stated enough, gift giving can be material or non-material. Social scientists Murstein, Cerreto, and Macdonald point out in their classic article, "A theory and Investigation of the Effect of Exchange Orientation on Marriage and Friendship," is that there are basically two kinds of people when it comes to exchanges. (And gift giving is certainly an exchange.) The first type is what they call the High Exchange oriented or E individual. This person feels uncomfortable if someone does him or her a Favor and he or she is unable to repay it. I see giving someone a gift in the category of doing someone a favor.

At the other end of the spectrum is the NE or non-exchanged oriented individual. These are people who could not care less if someone has done something for him or her. They do not keep a mental balance sheet the way the E individual does. (Murstein et. al., August 1977)

Why am I sharing this information with you? Because you need to figure out if you are dealing with an E or an NE individual, and what you are like, to minimize the problems gift-giving or even partaking in shared experiences as friends can have on your immediate and long-term relationship. If you figure out someone is an E individual, you had better be prepared to give them a gift if you get one from them.

If you give a gift to a NE individual, be prepared that you might not get a gift back, or even a thank you, because that is not their orientation.

In both cases, someone's personality put s them squarely into the E or NE category. It is not about you or your relationship. It's their orientation to the world and to exchanges including gift-giving.

Ideally you will not take someone's celebration preferences personally since it may have to do with their upbringing, how birthdays were socialized in his or her house, and so many other factors. If someone is having a birthday celebration, for example, and he or she says, "Please, no gifts," you need to know if that friend means that or if it's just a polite thing to say and a gift would still be appreciated, even if it's a donation in their name.

Consider this statement by sociologist Barry Schwartz in his classic 1967 article in *The American Journal of Sociology*, "The Social Psychology of Gift Giving," "Gifts are one of the ways in which the pictures that others have of us in their minds are transmitted."

I caution you, however, to avoid taking that statement too literally. Friendship needs to be an exchange and it needs to be reciprocal, but what I wrote in *Friendshifts* and what is still true" — what is exchanged need not be exactly equal but both friends must feel that their friendship is reciprocal. Maybe you call more often than your friend, but your friend makes sure you get a "girls' night out" on your schedule.

Also, when it comes to gift-giving, make sure your friend welcomes getting a gift from you. I remember years ago I got a friend a beautiful blouse. It cost around $25 which would be the equivalent of around $50 now. Much to my surprise, my friend was displeased by my gift. It made her uncomfortable. She did not want to start a birthday gift exchange with me for whatever reason. I had to respect her wishes and I never again gave her a birthday gift. Fortunately, we are still friends, exchanging a Facebook message and usually send a birthday card through the regular mail.

What about regifting? I added a question about regifting to my friendship survey. I am looking forward to reading the responses. I know this is a challenging question and dilemma for me. Would I be insulted if someone regifted my gift whether it is to another friend, relative, or even as a donation? I don't think so. Afterall, it is hard to predict what someone will like, and he/she might even already have that gift!

How do you feel about it? Someone could want to regift because he/she does not want or need what a friend has given to him or her. Or it could be a more general resistance to anything "material." One of my respondents shared that she is into a serious decluttering and non-materialistic mindset, so she does not want tangible gifts anymore.

In conclusion, I want to quote from the article by Dutch social scientists and professors Aafke Komter and Wilma Vollebergh from *The Journal of Marriage and the Family*: "One of the most distinguishing features of gift-giving, then, seems to be the following: Gift-giving, though in many cases objectively fitting within a pattern of reciprocity, is subjectively felt to be essentially a noneconomic, spontaneous, and altruistic activity that is meant to communicate personal feelings." (Komter and Volleberg)

Now on to Chapter 2, "Birthday Festivities," one of the most universal ways that we have a chance, once a year, to celebrate our friends or to be celebrated.

Chapter 2

Birthday Festivities

Celebrating a friend's birthday doesn't have to cost money. It can be something as birthday!" or placing a phone call to say those magical words that most of us like to hear once a hear, or to have a birthday get together over a cup of coffee or tea at your apartment or home, or a local coffeeshop, or lunch or dinner out together or in a group.

You could send your friend a bouquet of flowers for her birthday, or even get tickets to a music concert that are more expensive than you thought those tickets would be, but that is optional and secondary to taking the time to celebrate your friends and friendship. Who was it that said the motto, "Do Something?" (Goodreads attributes it to President Franklin D. Roosevelt) For friendship, and for our friend's birthday, I would like to modify it to "Do something positive and thoughtful."

That something might be a card or a phone call, or you might have a tradition of exchanging gifts or even going away on an annual or semi-annual birthday friend getaway.

There are those who suffer from depression or anxiety from time-to-time or on a chronic basis. Letting your friends know that you care about them on their birthday is not going to solve someone's deepest emotional challenges. But it could at least for that one day let someone know that he or she is valued. It is a memory builder that might just help someone to get through more challenging days by reflecting on how he/she is cared for.

A Brief History

In this section, I am going to briefly summarize what I learned about birthdays when I was researching birthdays for my popular illustrated *Birthday Tracker & Journal,* published originally in both paperback and hardcover in 2011. Even though Facebook and now even LinkedIn tells you that someone you are connected to, including friends, is having a birthday, you may still want to know in advance if you need extra time to buy and send a gift or plan a trip or visit.

So, the tradition of the birthday boy or girl wearing a crown is said to date back to ancient Rome when, in addition to celebrating private birthdays, celebrating the birthday of past and present rulers had become a custom.

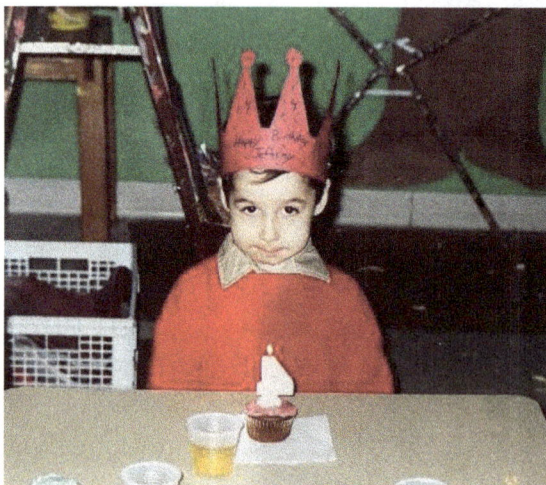

My younger son Jeff, who is now in his 30s, with a family of his own, wearing a crown at his birthday party, age 4.

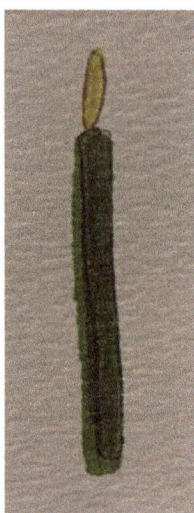

Some date the custom of a birthday cake to ancient Greece when a round honey cake or bread was taken to the temple of Artemis, the goddess of the moon. The custom of putting candles on a birthday cake is also said to have been introduced by the Greek because the candles enabled the cake to become more like the moon.

The introduction of more traditional types of birthday cake of a sweetened layer cake is attributed to Germany in the Middle Ages.

It is in Germany 200 years ago that the tradition of having children's birthday parties is said to have originated, called *kinderfeste (kinder* – children + *feste* – party in German).

Historian Elizabeth Pleck, in an interview about birthday parties published in the *Chicago Tribune*, noted that birthday parties started out as more elitest: "When birthday parties started out in the 19th Century, they were an upper-middle-class, elite, even upper-class idea." (Trestrail, October 8, 2000)

Courtesy of Shutterstock. Photo contributor Francisco Diaz Contreras

What about long-distance friends? How do you celebrate with them? A woman in her mid-sixties shared with me that she met her best friend decades ago when they both worked for a major company in Rochester, New York. She now lives in the South and she her best friend celebrate their birthdays with a phone call. They sing "Happy Birthday" to each other. "Sometimes for no reason at all we send each other presents and say it's an 'early' or a 'late' birthday present."

Birthday Celebrations Including Parties

My Mom, Gladys Barkas, holding a traditional birthday cake. She's wearing a dress hand painted by her sister Peggy.

Birthday parties have evolved into something much more mainstream. Inviting friends to your birthday party seems like a natural thing to do for many with relatives included as well. I recall attending a children's party years ago where there were only the child's or parents' friend. Not one relative was in sight. I asked my friend about this, and she explained she did that on purpose. She wanted to have a friend only party to avoid having a gathering that mixed her friends with her family.

17

In *Birthday Tracker & Journal*, I share what a woman in India told me about how her daughter Tara celebrated her fifth birthday. In summary, she got five cakes for turning five. She met with her four great grandparents and had lunch with her four grandparents. She had a tea birthday party at home with friends and she went to an orphanage with her grandmother where she gave out food and money. In a classroom, all one hundred girls sang to her. The next day, she had another birthday party with more friends and family.

Children, teens, and even adult birthday parties are an annual event that offers a chance to create friendship memories for us, our friends, and our loved ones. That might mean everything from just including one friend in a lunch together or a lunch plus movie outing. Or it could include a party with as many as forty friends and a custom-made cake that is such a work of art one wonders if it should be eaten. For one of my birthdays, six of my local friends and I gathered at a ceramics craft store where we all made ceramics objects.

For my older son Scott's ninth birthday, I stopped by the local pet store and scheduled a session with the owner for Scott and his friends and younger brother. It was a memorable 45 minutes of introducing everyone to a range of small animals including the one depicted here.

So, what should you sing to your friend when you celebrate her or his birthday? Do you have to pay a royalty if you want to sing the traditional "Happy birthday" song? This is a complicated answer because the original song, composed in 1893 by Patty and Mildred Hill, two sisters and schoolteachers living in Louisville, Kentucky, in 1935, 11 years after Patty Hill died, it got copyrighted. In 1989, Warner Communications bought the rights to the famous "Happy Birthday" song for $22 million dollars with the copyright extended until at least 2030.

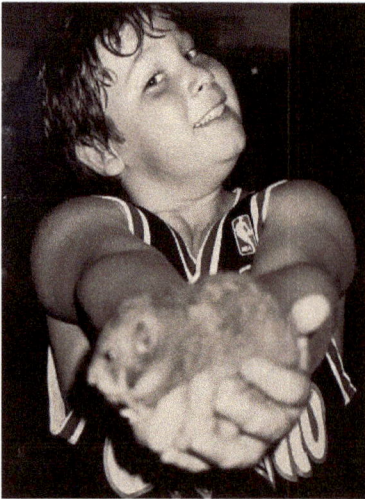

My son Scott's 9th birthday party with friends and small animal talk by local pet store

What you and your friends do for each other on your birthdays is completely up to you and your friends. The range of options is wide. It could be something as simple as a text and phone call saying "Happy Birthday" or something very lavish. If it is lavish enough it just might make it into the newspapers or on the Internet as happened back in 1989 over the weekend of August 19, Malcolm Forbes of Forbes Corporation gave himself a 70th birthday party in Tangier, Morocco. It is said that eight hundred guests were flown on a chartered jet and a Concorde plane including TV journalist Barbara Walter, former U.S. Secretary of State Henry Kissinger, and movie star Elizabeth Taylor, among other. The cost was estimated to be $2.5 million. (Emmrich, *New York Times*, February 15, 2017)

For my 70th birthday, my husband Fred, my friends Joyce, Mary, Robyn, Sharon, and Marcia, my sister Eileen and her husband Dick, and my older son Scott and his wife Lindsay, got together at a restaurant in Midtown Manhattan for a brunch. Might not have been Morocco, but it worked for me!

During the pandemic, I had a Zoom birthday celebration., It seemed like a better alternative to not getting together at all, but it was definitely different from getting together in person.

For Mila Johansen, celebrating her birthday with a friend is a ritual for her since she and her friend share the same birthday. As Mila, a writing coach and author based in California, explains it: "I have a friend who is a birthday twin. We try and celebrate every birthday together by throwing a fabulous dinner party. Sometimes we plan a getaway, often two hours away at Lake Tahoe, where we hike, swim, and eat out as many times as we can."

I conclude this little introduction to birthdays with the suggestion that if you and your friends care about each other, you just do "something." Birthdays are important whether you are twenty, forty, seventy, ninety...whatever your age! It is the day we enter the world, take our first breath, and our journey began. When I give a book to a newborn or infant, I often write in the front, "Welcome to the World!"

Photo of a birthday cake by an unknown author is licensed under CC BY-SA, Courtesy of Microsoft Word

Cards

It is convenient to post on someone's Facebook Timeline and if you are the birthday boy or girl it can be fun to see how many do post to your Timeline. It is also free and if you remember to do it on time, it can be a very convenient way to mark your friend's birthday, whatever their age. But you may also want to send an old-fashioned greeting card through the mail, or you might want to send an electronic card. As you will find out in Chapter 5, "Annual Friendship Events," one of those events was started by the Hallmark Cards greeting card company decades ago. They are still around and selling all kinds of cards as well as other greeting card companies including American Greetings, based in Cleveland, Ohio, and Vida & Co., to name a few. Blue Mountain, a company founded by artist and writer Susan Polis Schutz, was sold in 1999 and again in 2001 to American Greetings. 123greetings.com is another popular online greeting card company.

American Greetings also has an online e-card option. Another online card company, Jacquie Lawson, has cards that you can add music to.

You can make a card on your computer or buy one at the store in a range of prices. The types of cards available today for birthdays are for practically every type of relationship including birthday cards just for a friend!

You can make a card on your computer, or draw it by hand, if you are so inclined. You can e-mail or scan in and e-mail your creation or send it through the regular mail.

You will read more about gifts and other experience ideas in Chapter 3, "Gifts for a Friend for Any Occasion" including a birthday!

Chapter 3

Gifts for a Friend for Any Occasion

In this chapter we will explore different gift ideas for a friend. It could be for a birthday, or it could be for another occasion, or just to say, "Thank you for being my friend!"

Courtesy of Shutterstock. Contributor: Anna Tryhub.

With Words Including Essays, Poems, and Books

Celebrating friends with words can take many forms, an e-mail, in a Facebook post, in a poem you compose, handwritten on a commercial card that you send—or you could share a copy of a published essay on friendship or a book about friendship. You can also give books that have nothing to do with friendship but contain words and worlds you want to share with your friend or friends. Here are a few ways to use words when celebrating friendship.

Essays on Friendship

Some of my favorite essays on friendship include: Sir Francis Bacon's, "Of Friendship," Montaigne's, "On Friendship," and Ralph Waldo Emerson's, "0n Friendship." The Francis Bacon essay is contained in a collection of his major works, edited by Brian Vickers, and published in 2008 by Oxford University Press under the title, *The Major Works.* You can find the Emerson and Montaigne essays in various collections by major publishers or independently published by various individuals or companies. Just that essay is in the book entitled, *On Friendship,* published by Penguin Books in 2005 as part of their Penguin Great Ideas series. It is translated by M.A. Screech.

What struck me when I was researching friendship for my sociology disseration and discovered Montaigne's essay for the first time was how timeless it was, back then in the early 1980s, and even now. Consider that Michel de Montaigne was a Frenchman who lived from 1533 to 1592 and wrote a timeless essay that was published in 1580. His essay on friendship was supposedly inspired by the death of his beloved friend, Etienne LaBoetie, a lawyer and poet who died from an illness when he was only 32. In Montaigne's famous friendship essay he writes, "If a man should importune me to give a reason why I loved him; I find it could not otherwise be exprest, than by making answer: because it was he, because it was I."

To contribute such an eloquent thought, restated so often over these many centuries, is a true testament to Montaigne's insightfulness about such an amorphous and complicated relationship. Just writing about Montaigne's essay inspires me to try harder to encapsulate my own feelings about friendship and bereavement, especially the strong feelings of loss I have felt since losing two of my dearest friends Sharon Fisher and Elia Schneider, both gone too soon from illnesses.

On a more cheerful note, these are just three of the many essays about friendship you could read and then quote from with your friends, in cards, in your texts, e-mails, or social media posts, or just as background reading to help you challenge, or reinforce, your own views on friendship.

Poems

There are many books containing poetry about friendship. Unfortunately, a lot of those poems are not as memorable as I would like them to be. So, you might even consider writing a poem of your own.

There are some excellent collections of writings on poetry, including *The Norton Book of Friendship*, edited by Eudora Welty and Ronald A. Sharp, and published by Norton. If you look in that collection you should find at least one or two poems that might be fun to send to your friend, inside a card or along with another gift.

Here are a few of the many books with poetry related to friendship to know about. The first is for children and the second for adults of all ages: *I Like Being Me: Poems About Kindness, Friendship, and Making Good Choices* by Judy Lalli, published by Free Spirit Publishers, revised in 2017; *Poems on Friendship*. Signature Select Classics. Published by Union Square & Co in 2022. This book includes poems by such notables as Emily Dickenson, Henry David Thoreau, and Shakespeare. Since the poems by such long gone writers are no longer in copyright, you could quote from or reprint any of those poems to share with your friends.

Here is the part of *The Prophet*, first published in 1926, by Kahlil Gibran (1883-1931), a Lebanese American author, about friendship:

And a youth said, Speak to us of Friendship.
  And he answered, saying:
  Your friend is your needs answered.
  He is your field which you sow with love and reap with thanksgiving.

And he is your board and your fireside.

For you come to him with your hunger, and you seek him for peace.

When your friend speaks his mind you fear not the "nay" in your own mind, nor do you withhold the "ay."

And when he is silent your heart ceases not to listen to his heart;

For without words, in friendship, all thoughts, all desires, all expectations are born and shared, with joy that is unacclaimed.

When you part from your friend, you grieve not;

For that which you love most in him may be clearer in his absence, as the mountain to the climber is clearer from the plain.

And let there be no purpose in friendship save the deepening of the spirit.

For love that seeks aught but the disclosure of its own mystery us not love but a net cast forth: and only the unprofitable is caught.

And let your best be for your friend.

If he must know the ebb of your tide, let him know its flood also.

For what is your friend that you should seek him with hours to kill?

Seek him always with hours to live.

For it is his to fill your need but not your emptiness.

And in the sweetness of friendship let there be laughter, and sharing of pleasures.

For in the dew of little things the heart finds its morning and is refreshed.

Source: From *The Prophet* (London: Heinemann, 1926, pages 69-70). This poem is in the public domain.

Books and Books into Film

There are so many wonderful books, essays, poems, TV shows, and films dealing with friends and friendship, this just a small sample. I am sure you have many of your own favorites. This collection might offer you some options that you want to explore.

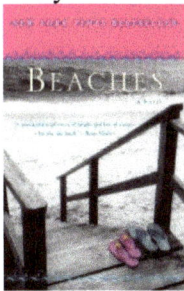

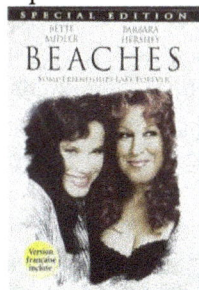

Beaches by Iris Dart, originally published in 1985, is a *New York Times* bestseller about the friendship of two very different friends, with the novel starting in 1951 when the two friends meet on a beach in Atlantic City and ending in 1983. between became a hit movie starring Bette Midler and Barbara Hershey. If your friend has not yet read the novel, you can get her a copy along with a DVD of the movie or a gift card to enable her to download it on a streaming service.

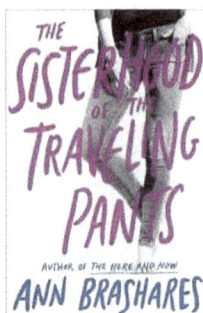

The 2005 movie version of this mega-bestselling YA (young adult) novel by Ann Brashares published in 2001, *The Sisterhood of the Traveling Pants*, is about how four best friends decide to use the sharing of a pair of pants as the way they will stay connected. In the novel and the first movie, the girls are all fifteen, turning sixteen before the summer ends. A sequel to the first movie was released in 2008.

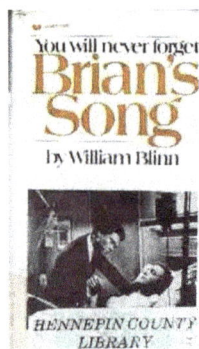

There was a TV movie in 1971 about the real-life friendship between teammates Brian Piccolo, played by James Caan, and Gale Sayer, played by Billy Dee Williams, about what is considered the first interracial roommates in NFL history and Sayer's death from cancer at age 26. Sayers died in September 2020 at age 77. A *Washington Post* article, "Gale Sayer's Speech in 'Brian's Song' is an essential Piece of Sports-Movie history," by Matt Bonesteel published when Sayers died does say that although they were friends, their friendship was exaggerated in its importance to Piccolo in the movie. As Bonesteel writes, "Truth be told, Sayers and Piccolo were close during their time together on the Bears...but not best friends."

Here are a couple of novels published by my company, Hannacroix Creek Books, that you might not have heard about that have a friendship theme. *Lucky the Orphan* by Ray Fisher and Dave Koco is a quick but memorable read about a group of kids who become friends when they all find themselves growing up in an orphanage. It's available in e-book, print, and audiobook formats. The co-authors are two expats from Pennsylvania and New Jersey, respectively, who now live and work in Tokyo.

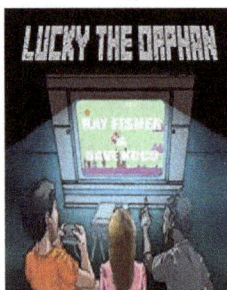

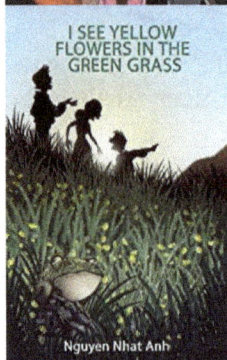

Hannacroix Creek Books also published the English translation of a middle school novel, *I See Yellow Flowers in the Green Grass,* that was a bestseller in Vietnam by Nguyen Nhat Anh.

The list of nonfiction or fiction books about friendship is voluminous. There are more than 800 entries in the selected annotated bibliography on friendship that I wrote and that was published in 1985 by Garland Press: *Friendship.* Imagine how many more books and articles there are now. When I first started researching friendship in the late 1970s, it was a topic that was getting far less attention by sociologists than parent-child or romantic relationships. But that has changed over the decades and now there is a plethora of books by not just sociologists but psychologists, workplace experts, and novelists, about all aspects of friendship.

You will find selected additional listings in the Works Cited and Further References section in the back of *Celebrating Friends & Friendship.*

Books are a wonderful gift for our friends, and it does not have to be on the topic of friendship, or a novel with friendship as an element in the storyline. In addition to encouraging reading, whether it is through an e-book, print, or audiobook version of a book, especially if you gift a book that you have read and enjoyed, it is another way of connecting intellectually and emotionally with our friends through literature. If you have a favorite book that helps people going through an experience in their lives, such as *Tuesdays with Morrie*, by Mitch Albom, which has helped millions deal with terminal illness and death, consider getting a couple of copies of that book to have on hand to send out for a birthday or if the occasion arises.

Thre is overlap in the category of films to give as a gift which today might mean a gift card to a streaming service unless you know your friend still has a DVD or Blue Ray player, since so many films are basd on books! Books are usually a solitary experience, but the film basd on the book can be a shared experience and if a book is an audiobook, you could have a friend or friends come over to listen to the book together. (See the discussion about TV Shows, Streaming, and Films that follows.)

However, the book you give to a friend does not have to have the theme of friendship as part of tthat book. You do, however, want to try to discover what kind of books your friend likes to read. Without giving away that you are buying him or her a book for either a birthday or another occasion, like the holidays, or no occasion at all, ask your friend what books he or she has read recently. Also, since I have discovered that readers tend to have a very strong preference for the format that they read it – e-book vesus print versus an audiobook – find that out in advance as well. You can gift all three although you will find it easier to gift the print version of a book. But you can gift an e-book or an audiobook by giving someone a pre-paid gift card for that item. You might, however, want to print up a "coupon" that you include in an e-mail or a card that you mail that announces they have a pre-paid book in e-book or audiobook format now available for them.

HAPPY BIRTHDAY

You have a pre-paid audiobook of
_____ (fill in the title)
available for you at _____ (fill in
the way that the pre-payment can be redeemed, such as
audible.com or itunes.com)
Just use this code: _____ (fill in)
To redeem your book! Enjoy!
Love,

If you give a print book, if possible, sign it in the front of the book, date it, and write something to your friend so he or she will keep it long after the first reading.

Music

"In the old days" you could send your frend a record, tape or CD of a favorite peformer as a gift, and some still do. One of the leaders for doing this is CD Baby.

But for most, music sharing has gone online with some of the most popular sites including Spotify, Apple Music, Amazon Music, to name just a few. If you want the sharing to be a gift, you can purchae a gift card for your friend for most sites. Usually it will be for a specific amount of money rather than for a specific performer or album.

Who are your favorite recording artists? Do you know who your friends like to listen to? Use the space below to find out and write down that information since it might be useful to you for giftgiving to your friends at their birthday, holiday, or for one of the annual friendship events you'll read about in Chapter 5.

Friend	Favorite performer #1	Favorite performer #2	Gift-giving record

In addition to gifting your friend the actual music,you could gift him or her something to play it on whether that is a computer or a smartphone, mentioned below in the Technology gift section.

If your friend has an interest in classic LPs, or even getting new LPs – even Taylor Swift is releasing her music on vinyl LPs these days – you could get yur friend a record pllayer if she or he needs one, or even one of the all in one music systems that includes a record layer, CD player, radio,and even a cassette player. Several years ago, back in 2020, I bought myself this record player that combines al lthe functions in one place. If you hve a friend who has LPs, or is considering purchasing some, and who also likes to listen to the radio, and old-fashioned CDs and cassettes, this multi-function system might be a gift your friend will appreciate.

Victrola multi-function music system.

TV Shows, Streaming, and Films

During the ten years *Friends* was on network television, from 1994 to 2004, and since that time, in reruns, streaming on the Internet, this show about a group of friends living in New York City, became for millions not just in the U.S. but aorund the world, their fantsy about friendship.

When Matthew Perry, one of the original cast members, died at the age of 54 in October 2023, allegedly drowning in his hot tub, the outpouring of grief from fellow cast members and fans emphasized just how important *Friends* and its stars were to so many. As the surviving cast members – Courtney Cox, Jennifer Aniston, Lisa Kudrow, Matt LeBlanc, and David Schwimmer said in a joint statement, "We were more than just cast mates. We are a family."

Friends is just one of the many TV shows with friendship as one of the themes of the show, on top of its occupaional setting, like *Grey's Anatomy, Will & Grace, Seinfeld, Two Broke Girls, Saved By the Bell, Living Single, The OC*—and what about all the realityTV shows that have a friendship theme? Like *Real Housewives of New York*, or *Real Housewives of Miami, Real Housewives of Beverly Hills, Real Housewives of New Jersey, Real Housewives of Salt Lake City,* and more.

Watching a TV show, or a streaming series, with a friends theme is a shared activity for friends whether it's a new show or reruns available through a streaming service.

Celebrating Our Friends with Flowers

1Acrylic painting on canvas with bow as collage element by Jan Yager.

Many of us, including me, grew up associating flowers with romantic occasions, like Valentine's Day, or wedding anniversary. But flowers can be sent to our friends for a special occasion, like a birthday, or just to say "hi, I'm glad we're friends."

Years ago, I had a party and one of my old friends from high school attended. She brought me such a beautiful bouquet that I was inspired to do a painting of that bouquet so I would have a permanent memory of it. You can always take a picture of any flowers your friends send you to preserve the memory forever if you don't paint.

Here is a list of flowers (reprinted from *Birthday Tracker & Journal*):

January – carnation or snowdrop
February – Iris
March – daffodil
April – daisy or sweet pea
May – lily of the valley
June – rose

July – larkspur
August – gladiolus or poppy
September – aster or morning glory
October – marigold
November – chrysanthemum
December – poinsettia or narcissus (daffodil or jonquils)

Here is another list of seven flowers according to Botanica Flora + Home of Portland, Oregon that are especially associated with friendship:

Photo credit: Jan Yager

Alstroemeria (Peruvian lily)
Zinnias

Sunflowers

Gerbera Daisies
Yellow Roses

Tulips

Daffodils

Yellow rose courtesy Microsoft Word through Creative Commons

28

Plants

In an ideal world, plants will last longer than flowers but make sure

Since flowers don't last forever, I like to take a photograph of the flowers as a permanent reminder of my friend's thoughtfulness. Sometimes I have even been made a collage or painting from the flower arrangement. I also sometimes keep the little gift card that accompanies the flowers as a keepsake.

Plant drawing on brown paper, created with markers. Artist: Dr. Jan Yager

your friend is a "plant person" and be careful about purchasing and gifting a plant that could be harmful to any pets or young children in your friend's home. For plants, as well as for other possible celebration ideas on this list, especially nuts because of possible allergies, do your research.

If you know your friend is very busy but would appreciate a plant, consider getting a plant that requires minimal watering or care.

Jewelry

Younger girls may make and give each other friendship bracelets but it became a new popular culture phenomenon when trading bracelets at Taylor Swift concerts became a tradition, according to CNN, inspired by the lyric in the Taylor Swift song, "You're on Your Own, Kid" from her Midnights album. (Samantha Murphy Kelly, September 25, 2023).

Assorted homemade friendship bracelets.
Courtesy of Shutterstock. Photo contributor Dudzenich

If friendship bracelets are not your thing, you can go online or visit jewelry stores and see what they have that is specifically for a friend or just a nice bracelet, necklace, or earrings that would be a welcome gift from a friend.

You can gift your friend any kind of jewelry you think she or he would like and that is within your budget. It does not have to be specifically for a friend. But if you do want something that has "friend" or "friendship" as part of the gift, there are many examples of this at online retailers in a range of prices. From bracelets to necklaces to earrings. You can also engrave some of the jewelry with your friend's name.

Do the necessary research to make sure the jewelry you are getting your friend will be something she or he will wear. For example, someone who has pierced ears may need a certain type of gold or silver in their earrings, such as 14K, 18K, or sterling silver. You also need to notice if your friend has pierced earrings or not. Someone with pierced earrings probably will not want a pair of clip-on earrings, however lovely.

Getting a necklace for a friend also means knowing how long your friend prefers for a necklace. There are lengths as short as 14 inches to as long as 22 inches. Of course, the longer the necklace, the more costly, usually, but if someone likes the necklace to hang down longer, getting a shorter necklace will lead to the necklace either sitting in a box, getting regifted, or requiring an exchange.

One of my favorite birthday gift years ago from my best friend Joyce was a jewelry box that she took the time to get engraved. There are jewelry boxes just for gifting to a friend with a slogan about friendship imprinted on the cover of the box or you can just gift a jewlery box and either engrave it yourself or keep it plain, but

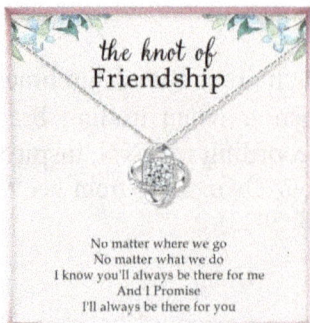

it is from a friend to a friend. You might also start off the jewelry box by including the gift of jewelry in the new box.

Here's a picture of a reasonably priced friendship-related necklace by a company named Diosky.

30

Birthstones

Here is a list of the birthstones for each month that might be useful if you want to get your friend jewelry*:

January – garnet
February – Amethyst
March – Aquamarine
April – Diamond
May – Emerald
June – Pearl, Moonstone
July – Ruby
August – Peridot, Sardonyx
September – Sapphire
October – Opal, Tourmaline
November – Topaz, Citrine
December – Turquoise, Blue Topaz
*Reprinted, with permission, from *Birthday Tracker & Journal* by Jan Yager (Hannacroix Creek Books, Inc., 2011)

> *"My bff (and her sister) once gave me a beautiful pair of diamond hoop earrings. There was no occasion, but I was sick with the flu and had been in bed for several days, and they wanted to cheer me up. I have them still and think of how they were given to me every time I wear them. Actually, I treasure them, knowing the thought behind my receiving them!"*—retiree in her 70s.

With Clothing

There are many clothing options to consider, from a kimono, costing as little as $10, to jeans or pants, to blouses, gloves, caps, hats, pajamas, or sweater. The list is endless and what makes a celebration of your friendship through clothing so thoughtful is that it is a practical gift as well.

You can also give a gift certificate to your friend's favorite store so he/she can buy the clothing. Or get a more general gift card for a one of the major credit card companies that issue gift cards in amounts as low as $10 or $25 and as high as several hundred dollars. You can also get a gift certificate for a particular brand that you know your friend likes that can be redeemed online or at a local brick-and-mortar store that carries that brand.

If possible, find out your friend's size in advance of ordering as well as your friend's color preferences. When in doubt, get a gift receipt for your purchase so the item can be exchange or refunded without much difficulty.

With Food and Beverages
Fruit baskets

You can buy a gift fruit basket from companies known for their fruit baskets, like Harry & David®, headquartered in Medford, Oregon, or you can even make your own. When my family first moved to Connecticut, a friend of a family friend in California stopped by to welcome me to the town. She put together a basket of fruit and some gourmet foods and I found it a very thoughtful gift.

Photo courtesy of Microsoft Word

Nuts or Popcorn

As long as someone is not allergic, and if you know that he or she likes nuts, consider a gift of nuts to celebrate a friend. You can buy nuts locally and ship yourself or use one of the companies specializing in nuts including Nuts.com.

This Photo by Unknown Author is licensed under CC BY-NC (Courtesy of Microsoft Word)

Popcorn is another way to celebrate your friends. If you're separated by distance but you still watch a movie simultaneously over the Internet, sending your friend popcorn could replicate what you used to do when you attended movies in person together. Or maybe you live close by so you can still watch movies or TV together or you are celebrating during your friend's getaway. There are many companies selling popcorn online including The Popcorn Factory and you can also purchase it locally and ship it yourself.

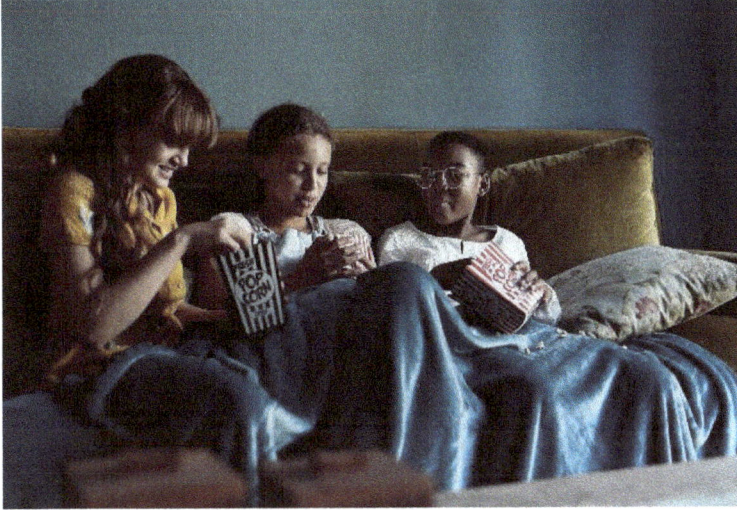

Chocolate

Just as flowers are not just associated with romance, chocolate is also a gift for platonic friends. A favorite for many is chocolate covered strawberries, the mainstay of Sherrie's Berries, although there are other companies that make these treats. You can also make your own chocolate dipped strawberries.

If you know your friend likes a certain kind of chocolate, such as dark chocolate instead of milk chocolate, how positive to gift her or him what is his or her preference. The range of chocolates is vast in terms of quality and cost but the key point to this inclusion of chocolate as a friend gift idea is that it is no longer just for romantic relationships.

Wine, Champagne, and Other Beverages

This can be an ideal gift for a friend who enjoys wine but even if your friend is not a wine drinker, he or she might welcome this as a gift to serve for guests.

For advice about wine as a gift for a friend, I turned to Karen B. Jensen, a Denmark-based expert on wines, owner of Distinguished Wines. Here is her reply:

For the friend who doesn't know anything about wine, but you know that your friend likes wine, although not sure which wine, then one possibility is to go to a nice bottle shop and ask if you could get a suggestion to a wine for your friend and remember that there are great wines in many price ranges. Good wine doesn't have to cost a fortune.

If you know your friend enjoys vegan or organic food, you could choose an organic and/or vegan wine which I am sure your friend will appreciate.

If you are looking for a wine during the summer it can bring joy choosing a rosé, a sparkling or a white wine that goes with many light summer dishes such as veggies or fish, or simply as a companion on the patio on a great summer's night.

If it is cold and wintery I would probably go for a red wine for my friend who can enjoy those precious drops with a meal together with friends and family.

If you haven't had the chance to look at your friend's wine rack or haven't received any suggestions from their family or friends, then you can also choose to be on the safe side and bring a bottle of white and a bottle of red that can bring joy on any occasion with friends and family.

Tea, Coffee, or Hot Chocolate

You could celebrate your friend with a special tea, coffee, or hot chocolate but as with nuts or plants, even if you know your friend a long time and you think she or he enjoys a particular beverage, he or she may have swished lately. Some tea or coffee companies have gift assortments that you can send so your friend gets to sample many new options. Hot chocolate, especially around the holidays, is often packaged with a mug and a little spoon and possibly even marshmallows.

Many companies, such as Bigelow Tea Company, which has been selling tea since 1945, have gift sets with assortments of tea. There are also gift sets of assorted coffees for a friend who enjoys trying new flavors.

Mugs

The previous category of viable celebratory gifts leads in nicely to this possibility: a mug. There are just so many mugs you could send a friend to celebrate her or him. You could even make your own mug through any of the imprinting companies. (See the Resources section for a few listings.)

What is nice about giving a friend a mug is that it is a relatively inexpensive and a practical gift. furthermore, if your friend drinks tea, coffee, hot chocolate, or another hot drink, or even chooses to use the mug to drink water, it is a daily or regular reminder of you and your friendship.

Mug that was a recent birthday gift from my friend Robyn

In addition to choosing from slogans like "I wish you lived next door" or "This mug is a hug from me to you" you can make-up and imprint your own slogan. You can even personalize the mug with your friend's name and your name as well if the spirit moves you. I recently created a generic "Thanks for being my friend" mug that I plan to customize with artwork and a friend's name at some point.

Other Assorted Gifts Including Donations, Gift Cards and Certificates

Hot Plates

This is another gift idea that can be a daily reminder of your friendship. The size of the hot plate could range from a larger size so it can be used in the kitchen or dining room underneath a hot dish at mealtime. It could also be a smaller size to fit underneath a mug for tea, coffee, or another hot drink.

Below is a picture of the hot plate given to me by my friend, the late Lucy Freeman. Lucy was an award-winning mental health writer for *The New York Times*, as well as a prolific book author whose titles included her best-known title *Fight Against Fears* (1951), and we became friends through our membership in the American society of Journalists and Authors (ASJA), which used to be called the Society of Magazine Writers. Lucy was a lot older than me by a couple of decades. When my sons were in school so I could take the train into New York City from Connecticut for a couple of hours before I had to meet the school bus, I would visit Lucy for lunch at a restaurant or we'd meet at her apartment which was on Central Park South. I enjoyed those get together and I know Lucy did as well.

4"x4" square ceramic hot plate for a mug, a gift from my friend Lucy

As I was leaving one of our lunchtime gatherings, Lucy gave me a hot plate to use when I drank coffee. That was more than twenty years ago, and I have used that hot plate ever since. It is a reminder of that special friendship with Lucy who died in January 2005 from complications of Alzheimer's at the age of 88. That hot plate does more than remind me of my friendship with Lucy. It reminds me not to let me stop you from having a friendship with someone because you are very different ages.

Artwork

If you are an artist, you can give one of your works to a friend. Or you can buy art as a gift. If your friend has a favorite artist, you could consider getting her or him a nicely framed print of a cherished art work.

Collage of our summer home in Greenwood Lake, New York
for two years where my brother Seth often asked his friends
to join us for a weekend Artwork by Dr. Jan Yager

Paper collage of a woman on a train
Reading a book. Artist: Dr. Jan Yager

If purchasing original art of an emerging artist is something you have not done before, you could consider purchasing the print, signed or mass produced, of a famous artist that you know your friend likes.

Photo frames

Although anyone with a smartphone usually has pictures on that phone to show and share, many are still printing out selected pictures and displaying those pictures on a shelf or on the wall. If your friend is in that category, she or he might appreciate a frame for a photo. There are also several companies, including Keepsake Frames (https://www.keepsakeframes.com) that someone uploads the photo, and they frame it and ship it back. You might want to get a gift certificate for such a service so your friend can handle choosing the picture and frame that he/she likes.

Candles

The assortments of candles to celebrate a friend is vast. You might want to make sure your friend is a "candle person" and if she/he is, what kind of candles, with or without an aroma?

Courtesy Microsoft Word.

Handmade products including knitted hats or scarfs

If you like to make handmake apparel like scarfs or hats, your friend might welcome your thoughtfulness. If your talents are elsewhere but you like the idea of giving a handmade item, there are many local or online stores that sell handmade goods including Etsy, Shopify, and even eBay. Around the holidays and in resort towns, at the beaches, or even at your local flea market, you may find artisans selling their handmade crafts.

Puzzles, Board Games, or Cards

Just like with plants you want to make sure your friend would welcome a puzzle or even a board game. Puzzles offer a wide range of options in terms of how many pieces, from as few as 100 to 500 or even 1,000 pieces.

There are so many board games friends of all ages may enjoy from their formative years or have rediscovered such as Scrabble™, Monopoly, and of course card games are a perennial favorite with friends. I know a group of ten male friends in their late 60s whose weekly card game that has been going on for more than a decade. During the COVID epidemic, they switched to playing via Zoom, but have since gone back to their in-person weekly get together.

Stationery or Greeting Cards

I still like to write, and receive, letters and I also enjoy sending and receiving greeting cards. Some have migrated to the online greeting cards and that is an option as well. And there is also the option of a homemade card. Microsoft Word and the software that is part of a Mac usually have templates that you can modify to make a card without having to be a professional artist.

Electronics

If you can afford to give your friend electronics, and you either will not go into debt over it, or your friend will not feel embarrassed by your generosity, here is a list of just some of the many electronic gifts that a friend might welcome:

- A smartphone (iPhone, Samsung Galaxy)
- A computer (HP, Dell, ASUS, Acer)
- Headsets (Bose, Beats Solo,
- High speed scanner (Epson, HP)

Appliances

Especially if your friend is in need for something, appliances can be a welcome way to celebrate including:

- Coffee maker including fancier version that enable you to make a pot of coffee on the left and a single cup on the right, other models have timers so you can set the coffeemaker up at night and it will start brewing in the morning at the appointed time)
- Microwave
- Vacuum cleaner
- Cooker – all-in-one Crockpot
- Blenders to make smoothies
- Countertop composter

Donations

You can donate in your friend's name to celebrate. If your friend has a favorite charity or two, that could be an excellent place to start if you are wondering what charity to donate to. Here is a website that offers guidance:

Charity Navigator
https://www.charitynavigator.org

Here are just a few of the countless worthwhile charities to consider (in alphabetical order):
American Cancer Association

https://donate.cancer.org

Alzheimer's Association
https://act.alz.org

ASPCA American Society for the Prevention of Cruelty to animals
https://secure.aspca.org/donate

Feed the Children
https://www.feedthechildren.org

Save the Children
https://www.savethechildren.org

St. Jude CHILDREN'S Research Hospital®
https://www.stjude.org

Tunnel to Towers
https://www.T2t.org
This organization pays off the mortgage of first responders killed in the line of duty as well as creating customized homes for severely wounded veterans.

Wounded Warriors
https://www.woundedwarriorproject.org

Organizing a Donation Effort

If your friend has had something catastrophic happen and he or she needs help paying the bills, or your friend's family member has died and you want to raise money for the funeral expenses, you could organize a crowdfunding campaign on your friend's behalf. You may want to share your goals with your friend rather than assume your efforts will be welcomed. If your friend agrees with your donation efforts, it could be a welcome help in a time of need.

Some of the top crowdfunding services are:
- Gofundme.com

- Kickstarter.com

- Indiegogo.com

Gift Cards or Gift Certificates

There are a few key questions to ask yourself when it comes to gifting a gift card. The first is whether your friend likes them. If you know your friend appreciates a gift card, the next consideration is if the gift card is for a specific product, company, or service, or if it is for a dollar amount through such gift card providers as Visa or Master Card. The gift card could also be for a favorite store, like Trader Joe's grocery store, Amazon, Macy's, Barnes and Noble, a favorite local independent bookseller, the list goes on and on.

In addition to commercial gift cards, you can create your own and give someone a gift card for a particular service or experience that they might like (as discussed in the next chapter) such as a coaching session for everything from how to find romance to an hour with an professional organizer, a pre-paid trip to the hairdresser (or the salon does not have their own gift cards), singing your friend up for a movie subscription service or even several gift cards to attend a movie, as long as you know the movie theaters he or she frequents,

Other gift ideas?

What are some other gift ideas that you did not read about in *Celebrating Friends & Friendship* that you want to record for now or future gift-giving possibilities? Use the space below to write down those ideas.

_____
_____
_____
_____
_____
_____
_____
_____
_____
_____
_____
_____
_____
_____
_____
_____
_____
_____
_____
_____
_____

Chapter 4

Additional Ways to Celebrate –

With Experiences

Movies

Sketch by Nancy Batra

Going out to the movies is back in vogue for a "Girls Night Out" or a "Boys Night Out." Sometimes going to the movies with friends becomes a "happening." I was in Sydney, Australia for an author tour for my book, *When Friendship Hurts,* when the movie version of the hit HBO TV series *Sex and the City* (1998-2004) was being released on June 8, 2008. It was quite the happening with groups of friends making it a required "Girls Night Out."

More recently, you saw that happening with the movie *Barbie* and, not long after that, with the movie version of the Taylor Swift's concert tour, The Eras Tour, becoming the highest grossing concert tour movie ever bringing in an estimated $250 million. (*The Guardian* online, Associated Press, December 8, 2023) As noted previously in the section on jewelry, friends wearing friendship bracelets to Taylor Swift's concert and probably to the movie version of the concert as well had become "a thing."

Brunch, lunch, dinner, or just drinks before or after a movie with friends is a way to spend time with friends.

Concerts, Theatre, or TV Shows

We already mentioned attending the movie version of the Taylor Swift concert but going to concerts or to the theatre with friends is another traditional way to spend time with friends that has been getting back on track in popularity again in this post-pandemic era. Unlike the movie option, however, most of the time it takes planning to get tickets in advance for concerts or for a show. If everyone can make

43

that and even have a backup plan if one or more friends gets sick or has something come up so going to the concert or show won't work, this is a wonderful way to build memories with friends. For example, some venues have ticket exchange or donation plans so the tickets do not go to waste. Alternatively, one or more of the tickets that cannot be used could be gifted to another friend or resold at the same or a discounted price so at least the ticket is not wasted.

Getting tickets for a live event for a friend as a birthday gift is another popular way to combine the shared love of performers or specific shows with your friend and making it a birthday present or as part of one of the annual official friendship events that you will read about in Chapter 5.

TV Show Audience

You must check out if your local morning shows have a live audience as well, but you can send for free tickets to be in the audience of any of the live network shows that tape or are live out of New York City, Los Angeles, and even Stamford, Connecticut. Combine the show with breakfast, coffee, tea, or lunch, and you have a unique friendship experience. Here is a picture of my best friend Joyce and I at the Wendy Williams Show which ran from 2008 to 2021.

Cropped version of the picture that was on TV of Joyce and me in the audience of the Wendy Williams Show.

I recently chatted with a retiree who was on the "standby list" for the Drew Barrymore show which was being taped up the street from the college where I was teaching a course later that morning. She shared with me that this is the website to register to put in your request for free tickets to various shows that have a live audience (even if the show is taped): https://1iota.com

Library or Bookstore Events and Art Activities

In most cases, events at the local library or bookstore are free, and fun to attend with a friend. Some of the bookstore events, if the featured author is a celebrity or bestselling author, and if the event includes getting a signed copy of the author's latest book, may charge a fee.

There are so many events at libraries for you and your friend to participate in based on your availability and your interests. Events are not always tied to authors and books. There are events that teach about new technology, like AI, or how to get a job or get ahead at work.

Bookstore events are varied as well and could include a cooking session with a cookbook author, or a celebrity event moved to a much larger venue because of a large crowd.

If you are an author, especially if you are a new author, or a seasoned author who has not published a book recently, asking your friends to attend a library or bookstore event is part of the tradition! Having a wide network of casual friends comes in handy when you are asked by some of the bookstores to guarantee at least fifty people are going to attend your book event! You must be careful, of course, that you do not let her professional goal of having a successful library, or bookstore event conflict with your goal of being the understanding and caring friend that you know you yourself to be. Everyone is busy these days, even retirees, so you must invite everyone to your event, but you also need to be gracious if someone is unable to join you for whatever reason!

Art activities are another enjoyable way for two friends—or a group of friends—to share a meaningful experience. Many communities offer creative events such as *Painting with a Twist*, a guided painting experience founded in 2007 in Mandeville, Louisiana. The business was created to help the local community recover after Hurricane Katrina, a devastating 2005 storm that caused widespread destruction and claimed more than 1,300 lives in and around New Orleans.

Today, Painting with a Twist studios operate in many cities and states across the U.S. including Florida, Colorado, California, Arizona, Illinois, New Jersey, New York, Pennsylvania, and many more. (Visit their website for locations and more detailed information: www.paintingwithatwist.com)

Because the sessions are guided, no artistic experience is required. Canvas, paint, brushes, and an apron are provided, and participants are welcome to BYOB—wine, beer, soft drinks—snacks, cake, or food.

Friends can attend simply for fun or organize a group gathering for a birthday, bachelorette party, new baby arrival, promotion, or any occasion to celebrate together. I completed the artwork shown here during a two-hour event at the Tampa, Florida studio, and the time flew by.

Parades

Another free option is going to a parade together. Local ones are fun, or you can plan a trip to one of the famous ones like the Macy's Day Thanksgiving Day Parade in New York City every year. Which leads to the next section on Friend getaways since for many, attending the Macy's Thanksgiving Day parade in Manhattan could be a big trip nationally or even internationally. And what about the Mardi Gras in New Orleans or the Carnival of Brazil, including the Rio Carnival which gets an estimated 1 million plus visitors to the city of Rio de Janeiro.

Friend getaways

• Three friends from high school, now in their thirties, with the approval of their wives, spent the weekend in Vegas going to a concert and reconnecting.

• A divorcee in her early sixties and her friends from high school whom she connects with quite regularly spent a weekend as gust at the new weekend house of one of those friends.

• Single but dating, this woman in her late twenties took the six-hour flight to Iceland from New York for a long weekend with several of her close friends to celebrate their friend's 30th birthday.

Friend getaways can last a day, a weekend, or longer. It could be an occasional excursion, or an annual ritual. That is what it has been for Kirsten Krohn, a Westchester, New York-based actress and executive coach specializing in communication, who has been going on a "long weekend every year" for more than a decade with a group of 14 friends from college. Kirsten explains:

> I graduated from Cornell University over 30 years ago and a group of 14 women from around the country from varying aspects of our class (i.e. Not all from the exact social, academic, or religious backgrounds) get together for a long weekend every year.

> The traditional began about 14 or 15 years ago, on our fortieth birthdays, and is a cherished (calendar marker!) time spent that reveals something about each of us every time.

> We found that scheduling our trip for a Thursday through Sunday the first week of March works best for everyone's schedule. Over the years, we've been to Puerto Rico, California, Savannah, Mexico, the Dominican Republic, and other destinations.

The 14 of us have 49 children combined, live across 8 states and have had some incredible moments of support, charitable opportunities, information sharing, etc."

For Dr. Raman Attri, who is based in Singapore, friend getaways have held a strong place in his life. As Dr. Attri tells it about he and his two friends, Rakesh Puril and Pal Kaushal:

> *One is a childhood friendship (with Pal Kaushal) which already survived for 40 years and went strong despite living in different countries. Another one (with Rakesh Puril) stayed for 30 years, which started during college time. The three of us have had several fun-filled getaways for days and days together to the level that those became iconic memories That's how we used to celebrate our friendship.*
>
> *Our careers and professions led us to settle in different countries. As we approach age 50, we have decided to settle in the same country and begin our cross-country getaway springs again like nomads.*
>
> *Now this may sound like any other friendship-as-usual story, but the twist is that I have been permanently disabled for life since childhood. I could not walk. My friends have taken me to distant places by holding my hands to help me scale mountains and challenging terrains. Without them, I would have been confined to the walls of my room.*

Dr Attri (on the left) on a getaway in Autumn 1999 in the valley of Chamba province of Northern India with his friends, Rakesh Puril (on the right), and Pal Kaushal (in the middle). (Dr. Attri's crutch is on the ground next to him.)

Spas

There are those special spa friend getaways if that is feasible. As Australian writer Susanne Gervay shares: "I really do love a spa with my friends. It's something I either gift or just have a special time together. We laugh, share secrets and best of all, relax. There are so many gifts over time, but a treasured one is a joint spa with a massage, pool, lunch and all that delicious pampering over friendship."

Going to a spa together could include just a one-day spa visit or it could be for a weekend, for one or two days during the week, or for an entire week. It could be going together to a local spa or even making it a destination friend getaway combining travel and a spa visit. If you and your friend live far away from each other, picking a spa that is halfway between your two residences, or even deciding on a spa faraway that becomes your friend getaway plus spa, such as in India or Germany, for example, is a way for friends to spend time together as well as do some something that is hopefully relaxing and beneficial physically and mentally.

Some spas can be outside of your budget right now or your friends. Add on the cost of driving or flying and you just might have to plan this spa getaway a year or more in the future. If you do that, however, it could be a nice goal for you and your friend or friends, and something to look forward to.

Just Getting Together to "Hang Out"

Friends of all ages need to get together in person, if possible. Having a videoconferencing get together is better than not having a get together at all. But it is certainly not as rewarding as an in-person one. As Dr. Attri put it: "We no longer see people celebrating such moments where social media greetings and video calls have become the norm."

Fortunately, my research has revealed for many getting together with friends, especially with the intense years of the pandemic of 2020-2021 behind us, are happening, but this is a reminder to make the effort to make such a find get together happen. It is okay if you are not going to an exotic location together for a long weekend, or even traveling on a trip as two couples on an ocean cruise or to a resort, for even a cup of coffee or tea at the local coffee shop, or a lunch, or even dropping by each other's apartments or homes, is a way to celebrate your friend and your friendship.

If you have to drive or take a train or plane to get together, sometimes you need to be the one doing the driving or flying to keep your friendship going for a range of reasons from your friend having more time obligations than you, to your friend might not like to drive or her/his car is in the repair shop, or just a personality trait that he/she prefers others to come to his/her home or apartment.

However, you and your friends work out the logistics, getting together is for many one of the joys of friendship. Beyond social media and even phone calls or Zoom or FaceTime communications, getting together is a way of keeping a friendship going that those in lockdown during the COVID pandemic of 2020-2021 found out just how much they missed those in-person gatherings. As one of the mothers on the working Moms' list I belonged to years ago when I was first starting my research for my book, *When Friendship Hurts*, put it, you can't hug an e-mail I'm paraphrasing, but that was the gist of her wise comment.

Mom and Evelyn, a friendship from age five until Evelyn's passing at age 89 in 2012 (my Mom passed away a year later at 90).

But sometimes you just must be the one to make the trip. My sister Eileen and I made the hour or so drive with our mom from Connecticut, where Mom was now living, to Great Neck, Long Island, where her friend Evelyn Weinstein lived with her husband, federal judge Jack B. Weinstein. Mom and Evelyn had become friends when they were in kindergarten together in Brooklyn, New York. They kept up their friendship after they both moved to raise their families. Mom and Dad to Bayside, Queens and Evelyn and Judge Weinstein to Great Neck, Long Island. Since Mom could no longer drive because of health issues, we drove her so the lifelong friends could chat and have lunch together.

Meeting Halfway

If you live in different states, you could pick a state between you, or another destination state, to meet halfway. If you live in different countries, you could find a country to meet in halfway between you as well.

For many years, my husband Fred and I made the three-hour drive from where we live in Connecticut to where my best friend Joyce lives in New Jersey. I also took a bus from Manhattan and Joyce would pick me up at the bus station and we'd spend the day together. Then the pandemic hit, and everything got reevaluated and I also had an epiphany: why not meet Joyce half-way? So, I asked Google where half-way between our two towns would be and the first time, we decided on Edison, New Jersey. The next time, we decided on New Brunswick, New Jersey. But the goal and accomplishment were the same: we each drove around an hour and a half to an hour and 45 minutes instead of one of us having to drive three hours one way.

Sports

Those sports activities of childhood can find their way into the lives of adults of all ages. It could be the newest sport, pickleball, or such timeless ones as bowling, soccer, football, volleyball, tennis, or baseball, to name just a few. The idea that sports activities are meant to be shared with a friend is so engrained in our psyche that Harvard University professor Robet D. Putnam's bestseller, published in 2000, is called *Bowling Alone: The Collapse and Revival of American Community.*

Even running need not be a solitary event if you run with a friend. You and your friend might consider joining a local running club. Walking with a friend is another activity that combines exercising with celebrating your friendship with regular contact.

Attending a sports event together is a great way for those who are sports enthusiasts to create friendship memories on a one time or regular basis. You could even consider getting tickets together if you don't live nearby and finding time to have those in-person get togethers is not always easy. That way you'll know that you will see each other and share attending the games of your favourite team.

Parties (besides Birthdays)

The sixth question in my survey completed by 37 men and women throughout the U.S. and internationally was about parties, besides birthday parties. I was surprised that only 27% indicated that they have parties besides birthday parties for their friends. But the result might have been higher if I asked about all their friends. I restricted it to close or best friends and parties. Except for smaller dinner parties, as we all know, larger parties usually include casual friends as well.

That result, however, made me consider my own patterns in terms of parties with friends and I realized I have not been entertaining or having parties the way I used to years ago. Have you found that true for yourself or your friends as well? Going out in smaller groups has become more typical for my husband and me. The bigger parties that I have been invited to in the last decade, and attended, other than gatherings related to a major event, like a bridal or baby shower, or a wedding, tend to be connected to business. Of course, during the height of the pandemic in 2020, getting together outside of one's small circle of relatives and possibly a few friends was put aside. But once the restrictions were lifted, has there been a return to throwing parties like the ones I remember having during my formative years in Bayside, Queens where as many as 100 guests would fill every corner of our house and backyard?

I wonder if the growth of connecting through social media like LinkedIn, Facebook, or Instagram and even having big gatherings over Zoom has led us to want to connect in our personal lives with just a few friends at a time rather than by having a big party?

So how many do you need to have in one room to call it a party? In his article published by Michigan State University, Ben Chamberlain writes that research indicates five to nine is the best group size for a party. So maybe the trend away from huge parties to smaller gatherings is a positive trend. (Chamberlain, "The right size for any party")

But if you do want to have a big party with lots and lots of friends, and the potential cost is discouraging you, consider turning it into a potluck event with everyone bringing a favorite dish, homemade or store bought. That can certainly keep the cost down.

Perhaps another reason there may be a reluctance to have big parties today, especially if that means offering alcoholic beverages to your guests, is the liability issue. The word may be out that if someone gets into an accident on the way home from your party, most states today have something called a social host liability law meaning the victim of a drunk driver could sue the host or hostess who served the alcohol to the guest who drove when over the legal limit and got into an accident where some was injured, a car was damaged, or worse.

So, taking the party out of the house to an outside venue or restaurant with a party room, or having a home-based party that is considered a "sober party" or a "booze free" gathering are other considerations.

Major Events Including Awards

What are the major events we hope our best or closest friends will show up to and even those casual friends who want to show their support? Baby showers, wedding showers, engagement parties, weddings, getting an award, and that inevitable passing, a funeral or memorial service. Just remember that friends are not mind readers. What may seem like a major event to you may not be that big a deal to your friend so if you need your friends there, let them know that their presence at a particular event is appreciated. Be careful, however, that you consider the personality of the friend you share that self-disclosure with. If you say it to a friend who sees that as unwelcome pressure, rather than as a way of reinforcing that their time and effort attending that major event will not be taken for granted, unfortunately it just might fade or end a friendship.

In most cases you must be invited by a friend, or you need to invite your friend, to have her or him participating in one of those major events including getting an award. Sometimes the award is announced in a way that you could be surprised when a friend appears. That happened to me back in 2006 when I was honored by my doctoral college with an Alumni of the Year Award from CUNY Graduate Center. My friend Betty Sung showed up. Even though decades separated us in age —we were 24 years apart. I was 31 and Betty was 55 when we first met as graduate students in the Ph.D. in sociology program at CUNY—we became "fast friends" as students. Betty was already a revered scholar in the Asian American program at CUNY, but she wanted to get her Ph.D. Betty passed away at 98 in January 2023. She and her late husband were parents and stepparents to eight children.

The late Dr. Betty Sung surprising me by celebrating my getting the Alumni of the Year Award from CUNY Graduate Center in 2006. Photo credit: Fred Yager

Attending a friend's major event is not always an easy commitment to make. Even for such fabulous occasions as a wedding, there are issues of timing as well as cost, especially if it's an out-of-town or a "destination" wedding. One of the hardest challenges I have found in my decades of friendship research as well as my experiences as a friendship coach are to help friends and even former friends, and even myself, to practice forgiveness if a friend does not show up at one of those major events. It is one of the more challenging forgiveness requirements – not showing up at a friend's major event. He or she says it's because of economic challenges and then you find out he or she is going on a cruise the next month, or just bought an expensive piece of jewelry.

How our friends spend their money is subjective and up to them. They may not feel they can afford to spend the money or the time to get to an event because they are committed to spending their money or their time in another way.

I refer to my book, *When Friendship Hurts*, or the companion workbook, *Putting WHEN FRIENDSHIP HURTS to Work,* if you find yourself in this situation. You'll learn how you can at least try not to let a friend's turning down participating in a major event to be the "crossing the line" event that fades or ends a friendship. Too often, that's what happens.

In addition to time and money considerations, there can also be psychological issues at work. Those psychological issues may even be on an unconscious level. A friend who is conflicted about having children may find it hard to show up at a friend's baby shower. Or the friend who just broke up with a boyfriend, or is recently widowed, may find it hard to attend her friend's second marriage festivities.

Volunteering

You could celebrate your friendship by finding time to spend together and doing good by volunteering with your friend, either in your neighborhood, if you live near each other, or **combine volunteering with a friend getaway as you volunteer at**

This Photo by Unknown Author is licensed under CC BY-SA-NC

an orphanage in Europe or Africa.

Other experience ideas?

What are some other ideas that you want to add for celebrating your friend and friendship?

_____

_____

_____

_____

_____

_____

Chapter 5

Annual Friendship Celebrations

The Benefits of Formal Events

If you celebrate your friends and friendship throughout the year, and even every day, you may feel that adding another celebration is unnecessary, and that's okay. But if you lead a busy life and time seems to fly by and you realize you haven't gotten in touch with one or more of your friends lately, or you just like the idea of having something structured and annual to facilitate communication with your friends, this section highlights friendship-related events you might want to have once, every now and then, or even annually.

The first three are the most popular, based on the anonymous 10-question friendship survey I conducted with 254 men and women between the ages of 18 and 89 throughout the United States representing all major races and ethnicities using SurveyMonkey's Audience program. More than half (52%) had heard of National Friendship Day (July 30th), next was International Friendship Day, celebrated the first Sunday in august, which had 13% of the respondents saying they had heard of it. I was flattered to see the event I created back in 1997, International New Friends, Old Friends Week, previously called national New Friends Old Friends, Week, had 22 who knew about it or 9% of the respondent. It had one more who heard about it for about Women's Friends Day, September 14th, and National Internet Friends Day, February 13th, was also known by 9%.

After you read about those three events, you will also learn about half a dozen additional events, arranged chronologically, that you might use as the reason to send an old friend an e-mail, or a new friend a text message, or to suggest getting together with an old friend for a lunch.

I decided for the sake of organization, to list and describe the events in chronological order, with January as the start of the new year. The descriptions of the various events differ in length.

Use the Notes blank lined pages in the back of this book to plan out and record your annual friendship day celebrations.

Annual Friendship Events – In Alphabetical Order

Friendsgiving

(In the U.S., falls on the same day as Thanksgiving, which is always the fourth Thursday of the month, so the date changes every year)

If distance separates someone from getting together with family for this annual uniquely American holiday, or if there are other reasons someone wants to celebrate without family. a version of the holiday which has come to be known as Friendsgiving has evolved.

Hasson d. Barnes, a lawyer, recommends that if you're attending a Friendsgiving celebration you should "maintain ethical and professional boundaries even in social settings. Enjoy the festivities responsibly."

Good advice, especially if some or all the adults at Friendsgiving have one or more alcoholic beverages that might influence what is said or done at the event.

In 2020, a movie entitled *Friendsgiving*, written, and directed by Nicol Paone, with Jane Seymour and Malin Akerman, was released. By 2021, Friendsgiving had become enough of an alternative to the traditional family-oriented Thanksgiving that CNN published an article about it entitled, "How Friendsgiving Found Its Place in the Holiday Season." (November 21, 2021) The article quotes Dr. Amy Adamczyk, Sociology Professor at John Jay College of Criminal Justice who authored a twenty-page article, "On Thanksgiving and Collective memory: Constructing the American Tradition," that was published in the September 2002 issue of the *Journal of Historical Sociology* that still gets a lot of attention.

Referring to the rise of Friendsgiving as an option in the United States, Dr. Adamczyk was quoted in the CNN article as saying: "'Given the constraints of this holiday, people are finding it relatively manageable to replace (Thanksgiving) with (Friendsgiving)," she said, referencing the shorter amount of time off usually linked to the holiday, while adding that many people "are going to do the traditional thing in four weeks, at Christmas.'"

Galentine's Day
(February 13th, the day before Valentine's Day)

According to Stephanie Weaver, writing in Fox29.com, Galentine's Day became "a thing" back in February 2010 when actress Amy Poehler introduced the word in an episode of the TV series, "Parks and Recreation." According to Merriam-Webster's dictionary, Galentine's Day is a "day for women to celebrate their friendships with their lady friends."

The women in someone's life are to be celebrated which might also include sisters, cousins, mothers, or mothers-in-law. Galentine's Day just is not supposed to include any significant others/spouses.

Weaver lists these activities for Galentine's Day:
- movie nights
- sleepovers
- spa trips
- ice skating
- hosting cooking lessons

If this annual activity appeals to you, what are your ideas for a Galentine's Day celebration?

International Day of Friendship
(World Friendship Day) (July 30th)

Courtesy of Shutterstock. photo contributor: ilikeyellow

The exact origins of this friendship day are a bit confusing. Research indicates that this friendship day started in the 1960s by a card company. But it lost favor, supposedly, because it was considered too commercial a holiday. On the other hand, Kidskonnect.com, in a July 27, 2023, post, suggests that Paraguay by an organization called World Friendship Crusade founded by Dr. Ramon Artemo Bracho was first to propose the day in 1958. It is definite, however, that on April 27, 2011, after the United Nations General Assembly (UNGA) formally recognized International Friendship Day with a written proclamation, it got more attention again. At www.un.org, there is a page devoted to July 30, the International Day of Friendship. Under the heading, "sharing the human spirit through friendship," stating:

> "Our world faces many challenges, crises and forces of division — such as poverty, violence, and human rights abuses — among many others — that undermine peace, security, development and social harmony among the world's peoples.
>
> To confront those crises and challenges, their root causes must be addressed by promoting and defending a shared spirit of human solidarity that takes many forms — the simplest of which is friendship."

Khwan (Kanyarat) Nuchangpuek hosts a celebration for International Friendship Day for the clients of the language app that she co-founded, Ling App, and for her own friends. Khwan is an expat from Germany living in Thailand. Khwan shares about the importance of International Friendship Day which is celebrated on July 30th every year and her activities related to it: "We engage users with related content to International Friendship Day and activities online. These events are not exclusive to our users but represent bonding opportunities for our diverse team as well. On a personal level, friendships play a crucial role. Being an expat in Thailand, my friends here became my extended family."

Like all the special days, or even the entire week devoted to friendship that are listed in this part of *Celebrating Friends & Friendship,* this day is a chance to recognize a friend and what he or she means to you. The United Nations hopes that countries around the world will recognize this day and celebrate friendship, especially involving young people in events and activities fostering friendship and a Culture of Peace.

How will you recognize a particular friend or celebrate this special day?

_____
_____
_____

International New Friends, Old Friends Week
(celebrated annually starting in May 1997 for seven days on the Sunday beginning a week after Mother's Day is celebrated in the U.S.)

Previously known as National New Friends, Old Friends Week, this is the week I founded in 1997. I purposely chose it to begin the first Sunday after Mother's Day because I had become aware that even though I was lucky enough to still have my mother back then, other friends, colleagues, and relatives did not. Especially if they were childless and single, without a romantic partner, for them friends had become their family. It has been included in Chase's Calendar of Events every edition since 1997. You can read the blog I wrote about this week at my website:
https://www.drjanyager.com/international-new-friends-old-friends-week-7-days-of-friendship-celebrations/

Here is a list of the themes for each of the seven days of this annual friendship celebration week with a few ideas for how to commemorate a friend related to that theme as well as space to write down your own ideas:

Day 1 (Sunday)
Remember Your Old Friends/Friendshifts Day
- E-mail, text, call, or get together with an old friend you haven't connected to in a while.
- Subscribe to Facebook or Classmates.com and see if any old friends are there that you can connect to.
- _____

_____

Day 2 (Monday)
New Friend Celebration Day

- Is there someone at school, work, or in the neighborhood that you like and that seems to like you? Reach out.
- Join one of the friendship apps or websites listed in the Resources section in the back to make a new friend.
- When Aaron Wertheimer went on a solo trip to Uzbekistan last summer to explore his family's roots and ancestry, he had an 8-hour stopover in Tashkent, the capital. Instead of having to navigate the city alone, a friendly 26-year-old Tashkent native sitting next to Aaron offered to show Aaron around the city. Aaron was more than happy to accept. "Months have passed since my trip" notes Aaron, a remote copywriter for Marketing-Reel (https://marketing-reel.com/facebook), but he and his new friend "keep in touch" monthly via Whatsapp. Aaron hopes his new friend will be able to come to the USA. This day during this friendship celebration week is an ideal time to celebrate this new friendship again.
- _____
  _____

Day 3 (Tuesday)
Friendship and Work Appreciation Day

Sharing a meal at work. Courtesy of Shutterstock. Photo contributor: fizkes

- Invite a work friend to coffee, lunch, or an after-work drink. or meal.
- If you work in a group situation, organize a work lunch._____
  _____

Day 4 (Wednesday)

Be Your Own Best Friend Day
- Treat yourself to something you enjoy doing that you don't get time to do.
- Make a list of at least five traits that you like about yourself.
- _____

_____

Be 5 (Thursday)
When Friendship Hurts: A Day of Healing
- Work on stopping obsessing over a failed friendship.
- Allow yourself to grieve for a faded or ended friendship, focusing on what was positive when it lasted.
- _____

_____

Day 6 (Friday)
Children and Teens Anti-Bullying and Pro-Friendship Day
- Talk to your child about bullying – what it is, what to do if it happens to them or someone they know.
- Talk to your teen about bullying._____

_____

Day 7 (Saturday)
Finding the Time for Friendship Day
- Take out your appointment book and block out time for getting together with your friends.
- Remind yourself that you have enough time to get everything done, that's a priority so make sure you're making friendship a priority.
- _____

_____

Over the years, here are just some of the ways that centers, websites, individuals, and even the government celebrated International New Friends, Old Friends Week, previously known as National New Friends, Old Friends Week.
- An adult day care center in Florida scheduled an activity that week around the topic of friendship and *friendshifts*.
- For three years in a row, a website sponsored a Friend ship/Friendshifts contest. Prizes included signed copies of Friendshifts and friendship gift baskets. (Unfortunately, Neatwomaninc no longer exists as a site; its founder, Caryl Frawley, passed away.)
- Seventeen senior centers throughout Virginia highlighted friendship at their friendship cafés.
- A camp made friendship the theme for the entire week. It was so successful it was extended for the entire six weeks.
- A librarian at the Navy base in Yokosuka, Japan organized a luncheon program and suggested "take a friend to lunch" especially during that week.

I welcome hearing from you about how you are celebrating May's International New Friends, Old Friends Week. Although personal replies cannot be guaranteed, e-mail me at jyager@aol.com. (Please, no SPAM.) You can also share by using the "Contact Us" form at https://www.drjanyager.com

National Best Friends Day (June 8th)

This day supposedly was chosen by the U.S. Congress in 1935 to pay tribute to close friends. Here are some suggestions about how to celebrate this day:

- Communicate with your best friend via phone, text, or e-mail.
- Get together in person for breakfast, coffee, lunch, or dinner.
- Watch a best friend movie together. Some suggestions? Beaches, *Thelma and Louis, 9 to 5, The Joy Luck Club, Wayne's World, The Shawshank Redemption, Brides Maids, The Big chill, A League of Their Own, Steel Magnolias,* and *Lord of the Rings.*
- Go for a walk or run together.
- Exchange cards or token gifts.

  How will you celebrate?
- _____

National Friendship Day
(the first Sunday in August)

In 1935, the U.S. Congress declared the first Sunday in August to be celebrated as National Friendship Day.

Here's what National Day Calendar (www.nationaldaycalendar.com) wrote about this day: "On the first Sunday in August, National Friendship Day encourages people across the country and world to connect with friends. Make a new friend or reconnect with an old one." (April 30, 2014)

Suggested ways to celebrate this day celebrated throughout the U.S. and around the world:

- Reach out to your new and old friends and let them know that you care.
- Exchange cards or a token gift.
- Talk on the phone, send a text or e-mail, or get together in person.
- Use this annual event as a time for a scheduled friend getaway.
- If you can't get together in person, set up a Zoom call, or use another videoconferencing service, with one or more of your friends.

How will you celebrate?

_____
_____
_____

National Girlfriends Day
(August 1st)

We already mentioned National Best Friends Day, on June 8th, which could apply to males and females. This another annual celebration for friends with the focus on girlfriends. (You will see that there is also a Women's Friendship Day, on September 14th.

Here are some ideas for how to celebrate this day:

- If you live in the part of the world that is summer, go swimming with your girlfriends.
- Communicate with each other by e-mail, phone, text, or getting together in person.
- Watch one of the movies about girlfriends listed above in the National best Friends Day category.
- Workout together at the gym.
- Get a manicure or a pedicure together.
- Take a walk or a run.
- Have a girlfriend party.

How will you celebrate?

_____
_____
_____

National Internet Friends Day (February 13)

By the 1990s, the Internet was becoming a way of life for so many of us. By the 2000s, how we communicate with each other, and even how we made friends, was transformed by the Internet. I have always been fascinated by respondents or interviewees who told me that a male or female friend was made, and maintained, completely online. For *Friendgevity,* I interviewed a bestselling author. Loree Laugh, and her friend. Robert lives outside of Houston, Texas, and Lorree in Baltimore, Maryland. Their friendship started and continues online, and they both find that works for them. (*Friendgevity*, page 77)

There are others, however, who see the Internet as a way to start a friendship, but they want to take it offline at some point. Since one of my other areas of expertise is crime victimization, just be careful that you only move your friendship offline if you feel completely confident to do that. Also, initially, you may want to consider meeting in a public place and even asking another friend along.

You will find apps and websites for forming friendships in the Resources section in the back of this book. Because of time and distance, some of those friendships that start online may remain online. If you have one or more friendships like that, National Internet Friendship Day might be a day that has special meaning for you and your Internet-based friendships.

Here are some ways to celebrate:

- Consider using this day as a time to set up a Zoom call or to use another videoconferencing method in addition your Internet communications.
- Let your Internet friends know that they matter to you even if it is mainly or completely online.
- Send a traditional card through the mail or an online card.
- Send a gift.
- Get out some popcorn and watch a video or movie together.

How will you celebrate?

_____
_____
_____
_____

Women's Friendship Day
(third Sunday in September)

According to holidayinsights.com, in 1999, Kappa Delta Sorority, a sorority, started in 1897 in Farmville, Virginia, started this special friendship day. The sorority is said to have over 180,000 members.

If you take the name of this friendship day literally, it has a broader meaning than National Girlfriends Day since Women's Friendship Day could include friends of both genders. Here are some activities to do on this day:

- Go out to breakfast, lunch, or dinner together.
- Have a friendship party.
- Exchange cards.
- Volunteer together.
- Consider how women are being treated around the world and commit to helping wherever their rights are under siege because of forced early marriage, limited access to education, intimate partner violence, or the gender gap in wages.

How will you celebrate?

_____
_____
_____
_____

There are so many annual events for celebrating friendship you can spend many days and even an entire week in May every year celebrating friendship! However, you may still feel that there needs to be another annual friendship event that is formalized or that you and your friends will informally observe, such as:

- The day you first met, and your friendship started. Some refer to this as the *friendversary*.
- The end of your first year as friends and the beginning of year 2!

- Museum Day. So many of us want to go to a museum but we always find so many other obligations stop that from happening. If you and your friend both enjoy museums, you can establish an annual Museum Friend Day, so you know you'll both at least get to a museum once a year!
- Holiday shopping together. Especially if you have small children and you don't want to take them shopping with you so the gifts will be a surprise, plan a shopping trip with a friend so you can accomplish your task together.
- Black Friday as a friend tradition. One of my college students shared that she and her girlfriend have met and gone shopping on Black Friday in person shopping beginning in high school. It's become an annual tradition for them.
- Add your ideas here: _____

_____

_____

_____

Chapter 6

Wrapping Things Up

Being There for a Friend in Need

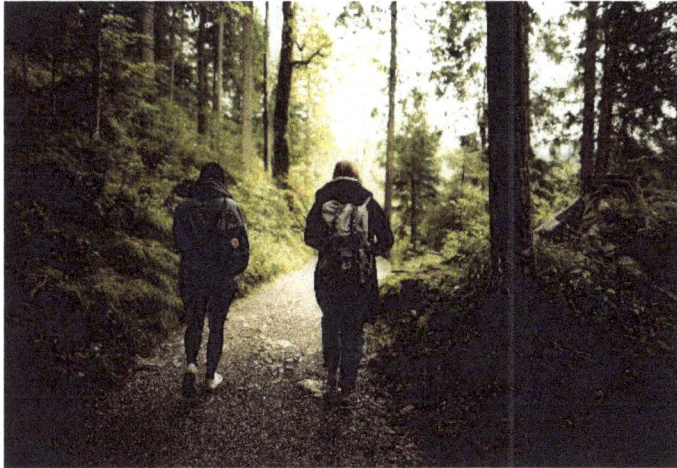

Courtesy of Microsoft Word, Creative Commons.

Indiana-based Faye shared with me about the challenge of navigating the Chron's disease that her "dear friend" has been battling for many years. As Faye notes, "It's a journey that has deeply impacted our friendship, turning it into a profound bond of empathy, support, and resilience."

A few years ago, Faye and her friend decided to start a business together. As Faye explains, "I find myself often reminding her to take her medication, eat healthy, and rest adequately."

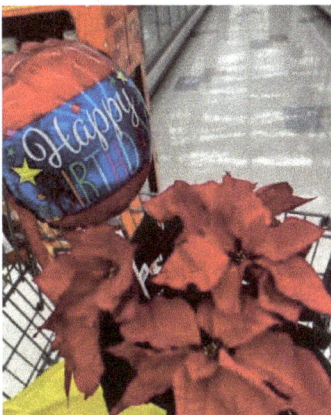

A welcome birthday gift to a friend's sister

Anyone who has been there for a sick friend knows the truth of what Faye shared with me: "These experiences have taught me the true essence of friendship."

Illness tests friendship and it is more important than ever to celebrate friends who are ill. I think of my wonderful best friend Joyce and how we brainstormed how she could celebrate the birthday of her close friend's sister who has terminal cancer. We agreed a beautiful vibrant red plant and one of those festive "Happy birthday" balloons would be a welcome celebration.

Another issue that tests friends in times of need is loaning money. This is a very controversial topic Just keep in mind that if you can afford to help a friend in need, do it. If it's a loan, write it up and have an agreement about the terms of the loan. But remember that if your friend has fallen on hard times, he or she may have every intention of paying you back, but it just might not be feasible right away if at all if getting back on his or her feet, keeping a roof over his or her head, is the primary objective. If you can afford it, you might want to gift your friend the money and then be pleasantly surprised if the money is returned, with or without interest.

The topic of money could be associated with gift giving if the situation arises where the reason for a gift is cancelled. Should the gift be returned? This was the question that a Newsweek reporter, Melissa Fleur Afshar, posted about in the online source for journalists and experts, Qwoted (qwoted.com) I answered the reporter's query and that led to being quoted in the article she wrote about the situation, entitled, "Woman Wanting Gift Back After Wedding Called Off Divides Internet: 'Cringe'" which was posted at Newsweek online, on November 20, 2023. Here's the situation in a nutshell: Someone wrote that she gifted her close friend for the last 15 years a chair worth $4,500 for her engagement. However, her friend broke the engagement and called off the wedding. Her other friends all suggested she should ask for the chair back. What was my expert opinion?

Now that you've read this entire book, you can probably guess what I suggested. Her friend is already grieving the loss of her fiancé, and the cancellation of her upcoming wedding, should she also have to lose this chair? I should add, however, that if the friend offers to give back the chair, or to give her friend some or all the cash value of the chair, that's a whole other issue. But to ask her friend to return the chair under these circumstances does not seem to be a friendly thing to do.

What do you think? You may be shocked that someone would spend $4,500 on a chair as an engagement gift in the first place, but that's a whole other issue!

If you treat any gift you give in the same way that I suggest you consider any monetary loans to a friend, you are less likely to hurt your friendship. But, as noted above, if the loan has a written agreement associated with it, that can be better for all parties concerned but you must decide, in advance of making the loan, what you will do if you friend is unable to pay back the loan in a timely fashion or at all.

Celebrating a Life

I read somewhere years ago that it is the things you don't do that you regret, not the things you do. That's an overly simplistic philosophy but, in most instances, that is true. When it comes to funerals and mourning the death of a friend, that has been true for me. *Closure* is an overused word, but whenever I do attend the funeral of a loved one, it does provide me with some closure.

That's why I'm including a section on how to celebrate the life of a friend who passes away. I felt guilty but I was too upset when my close friend Sharon Fisher died to attend her funeral. I did write a eulogy and a mutual friend, Nona, was gracious enough to attend the graveside funeral and read my eulogy so her two nephews – her parents and only sibling had died years before and Sharon was single and never had any children – would know how much her friend Jan cared for her.

I was too distraught to go, and I didn't think to ask my husband or another friend to go with me. So, my experience has been that if I am invited and I am able to go to a funeral, I feel better if I go than if I decline.

My friend David Friedrichs of five decades – he was a classmate of my brother, Seth Alan Barkas, at NYU in the early 1960s and a fellow criminologist, college professor, and author -- died a year ago and he left instructions to his adult children that he did not want to have a funeral. They could have a memorial which they did a few weeks after his passing so family and friends could meet and talk about David, and that worked out fine. David's wishes were honored, and the memorial gathering helped all of us who wanted to be able to celebrate his life.

I just did a search in Google on my late friend, David Friedrichs, leading me to his obituary at jenningscalvey.com. Toward the end of the summary of David's accomplishments and a list of his beloved family members, is this statement by my friend, who, even in his passing, continues to be an educator. It reads, "To those who want to commemorate his memory, David proposed the following: 'Take the time to do something you love, spend time with those important to you, explore things that interest you.'"

Celebrating the departed can also be done through scholarships in the name of the departed as well as even setting up a foundation related to a cause that a departed friend cared about.

There is another way we can celebrate our friends even if the major event is

something we are not invited to, but we are aware of it. This is what happened when my 97-year-old mother-in-law, Mary Yager, died from complications of COVID in October 2022. There was no funeral, but we did plan a memorial service the following month although it was going to be attended by mostly my mother-in-law's four surviving adult children, their children, and her great-grandchildren. Since Joyce lived 5-1/2 hours away in New Jersey, I wasn't even going to invite her to the graveside service near Albany. But Joyce surprised my husband Fred and me over the next few days when one of the biggest indoor plants I've seen arrived to mark the solemn occasion of my mother-in-law's passing. That plant was Joyce's way of letting us know that she celebrated my late mother-in-law and that she acknowledged the loss we were all feeling, especially Fred on the loss of his beloved mother.

If there is no funeral, or if the funeral is only for the immediate and extended family, you can still show support for your friend who has lost a loved one by sending a condolence card, donating to a charity in the name of their departed, or sending a plant or flowers.

In a previous chapter you read about *Beaches*, one of my favorite movies about friendship and about dealing with a friend's death. Everyone grieves differently and for some, seeking out professional help may be required. Compassionate Friends has friends in the title and it's a peer support group with chapters throughout the U.S. and internationally. There are in-person or online support groups. However, it tends to be focused on those who have lost a child or even a sibling.

Where do those who have lost a friend get help for their grief? You might have to work with an individual therapist. See the listings in Resources for BetterHelp and Talkspace, online and virtual services with licensed therapists, as well as through the referral directory of the American Psychological Association. If you know someone who has dealt with grief in therapy related to a friend's passing, you might ask for a referral.

Then there's the whole funeral or memorial service situation. There are some friends you may discover who just cannot deal with death in any way, shape, or form. They need to deny its existence and inevitability and they do that by avoiding being present at a funeral or a memorial service. Someone could invite her or his friend to the funeral of a parent or a spouse or another friend and that friend has an excuse about why he or she is unable to attend. It could be a great excuse like "I'm going to be on a business trip to another country" or it could be because of the emotional block to anything involving death.

Celebrations Do Not Have to Be Material

Not everything has to cost money or to be a material object to be a celebration of your friend and your friendship. Posting on LinkedIn, Facebook, or Instagram about how you feel about a friend you have lost or every just to have a shout out to a friend for his or her birthday, or applauding an accomplishment, can go a long way!

And you have seen in this book and in your own life that the experiences that we create or partake in with our friend or friends can cover a wide range. It is something free and accessible such as just getting together to chat, to taking a walk, to joining a regular sports activity or a book club for ongoing connecting, to such more luxurious friend getaways like a trip to Greece or India or volunteering at an orphanage in Africa.

The possibilities for free, low-cost, or more luxurious material gifts or experiences is vast. My goal for this book, and I hope I have achieved that goal, was to get you thinking more about celebrating in every way you can.

No way that we celebrate our friend or friends is too small or insignificant. As I showed you in the section on gifts in Chapter 3, that little hot plate from my friend Lucy Freeman has been on my desk for more than twenty years now. It is a reminder of my friend Lucy and of our friendship, that did not let many decades between us stop us from connecting as writers and as women. I predict Lucy was gifted that mug hot plate or she bought it for herself at some point. That she did not buy it or spend a lot of money on it was irrelevant to me. The cliché, "it's the thought that counts," could fit this situation but I prefer to try for my own slogan: "Celebrating a friend is what counts whether it is free or for a fee as long as it includes you and me."

I want to end this conclusion with a smile but with tears as well as I share with you, my dear reader, about my friends who I miss everyday:
I celebrate you, Sharon.
I celebrate you, Elia.
I celebrate you, Fran.
I celebrate you both Davids.
I celebrate you, Aaron.
I celebrate you, Irwin.
I celebrate you, Betty.

The friends I lost in just the last four years. My seventy-fifth birthday is on December 16th so I know, going forward, I will be adding to that list. So let me now celebrate those friends I have now who are with me still:
I celebrate you, Joyce.
I celebrate you, Robyn.
I celebrate you, Dara.
I celebrate you, Nona.
I celebrate you, Marcia.
I celebrate you, Mary.
I celebrate you, Paula.
I celebrate you, Monica.
I celebrate you, Gail.
I celebrate you, Sharyn.
I celebrate you, Linda.
I celebrate you, J. Barry.
I celebrate any friend who I left out of this list! Forgive me!
I celebrate _____, the new friend I haven't met yet.
I celebrate _____, someone I know who is becoming my friend.

I also celebrate my friends who faded or ended our friendship. You will be nameless but know that in the interest of Friendshifts, our time together, whether it was months, years, or decades, still matter to me.
What friend or friends do *you* celebrate? If you like, use this space to write down their names:
I celebrate _____
I celebrate _____
I celebrate _____
I celebrate _____
I celebrate _____
I celebrate _____

I celebrate _____
I celebrate _____
I celebrate _____

Some Additional Thoughts

You may be tempted to be offended by the failure of your friend to show up at a major event. After all, major events are one of the top ways we celebrate our friends and our friendships. Perhaps you gave your friend a birthday gift, but she did not reciprocate or even say "thank you." But my advice is to consider applying a very non-academic maxim to these situations: "Cut your friend some slack." There could be a good conscious reason your friend couldn't make it or didn't acknowledge or reciprocate your gift. Or even an unconscious one that she or he is completely clueless about. Consider the other aspects of your friendship. For example, if it is what I refer to as a "nostalgia" friendship, a friendship dating back so far that you simply can't make up those years that you shared. Do you want to consider discussing the situation if it really bothers you or can you let it go?

You do not want to be mistreated or taken advantage of or disappointed too often. If it's occasionally, that's one thing. If it's chronic, that is a whole other issue. As noted in Chapter 1, for most of us there is a need to have relationships and exchanges – material and non-material – in balance.

In Conclusion

To me, our friends are the people we have connected to throughout our lives for a short or a longer time who like and even love us, and we feel the same way. Friendship is a gift that needs to be celebrated in a non-material way, like letting our friend know we care by returning a text, picking up the phone and calling, or listening when you're super busy but your friend needs to talk. Or we could celebrate in a big way by going on a friend getaway together, sending a token or more substantial gift, or finding a way to get to that faraway special occasion or, if we can't, at least communicating how much we're disappointed that we can't be there. Maybe they're live streaming it so we should be sure to watch it!

As psychologist and college professor Marisa G. Franco writes in *Platonic: How the Science of Attachment Can Help You Make and Keep Friends*, "Our friends permit us to accept our flaws, to allow them to be a piece of who we are rather than our scarlet letters."

What is your biggest "takeaway' in this book? What idea or ideas most resonated with you? Here's a place to write those thoughts down:

My number #1 takeaway from this book is:

_____
_____
_____
_____
_____

Thank you, dear reader, for going on this celebrating friends and friendship journey with me. I appreciate each reader of any of my books. I do not take your time or interest in any of my nonfiction or fiction writings for granted. You matter to me!

I celebrate you, my dear reader, and I celebrate all our friends and friendship! Over these many years that I have been writing, and publishing, I have learned that my readers, even the anonymous ones, are an author's friend. It is a pact between every reader and a particular book and its author that in so many ways do resemble friendship. Like friendship, it is voluntary, it is not legally binding, and, like friendship, it should be valued whether it lasts for one sentence, a paragraph, for just one book, or for an author's entire canon of work.

I invite you to finish this book by filling in this sentence:

"I   celebrate   my   friends   and   friendship   because

_____

_____

How I Researched this Book

This book builds on research I have previously done for my books on friendship including *Friendshifts* and *Friendgevity,* as well as work relationships including friendship such as *Productive Relationships* and *Who's That Sitting at My Desk?* and even my related journal, *Birthday Tracker & a Journal.* Those books are listed in the "Works Cited and Further References" section of this book.

I also did additional research just for this book. I want to thank everyone who filled out my survey or who did an interview with me about friendship over the years but especially for this new book. In addition to an anonymous 10 question friendship survey that I distributed to 254 men and women through Survey Monkey's Audience program, I distributed a longer friendship survey to those who answered my queries on Help a Reporter Out (HARO), through queries posted in LinkedIn, Facebook, X, or in Freelance Success, or who I invited to participate in my research. As I go to press, I have received more than 50 communications regarding celebrating friends including 37 completed surveys and more than twenty e-mails from men and women throughout the U.S. and as far away as Thailand, Singapore, Australia, India, and the United Kingdom.

Here is the link to that expanded friendship survey that I created specifically for this new book that is posted online. I welcome hearing from you if you would like to fill out and submit this survey: https://www.surveymonkey.com/r/X5ZTSNH

FRIENDSHIP

Resources

Please note: Inclusion on the lists that follow does not constitute an endorsement nor should anything negative be implied if a resource is not included in this list. This list is for general information only. You are required and asked to do your own due diligence about any listing. Also, companies can go out of business, and websites can change or also disappear, overnight so the accuracy of any listing cannot be guaranteed.

Websites that sell gifts including imprinting products
Zazzle.com
Here is the link to my own store at Zazzle
https://www.zazzle.com/store/drjanyager_store

Vistaprint
https://vistaprint.com
Known for printing business cards, it also imprints mugs and photo books.

Printify
https://printify.com
a print-on-demand platform that enables you to create and/or sell a range of products on demand (one at a time).

1-800-Flowers.com
https://www.1800flowers.com
Founded by Jim McCann in 1976 when he opened his first floral shop in Manhattan. Over the years, it's expanded beyond flowers through its acquisition of The Popcorn Factory®, Cheryl's Cookies®, Harry & David®, Shari's Berries ® and other companies.

Associations, Agencies, or Companies
Counseling
Note: Especially because of the 2020 pandemic, even traditional in-person therapists have begun offering phone or videoconferencing sessions.

There is a wide range of professional help available to you through traditional in-person counseling or through phone, text, e-mail, or videoconferencing. That includes psychologists, psychiatrists, social workers, and pastoral counselors. In this section, you will see the listings for associations where you can find professional therapists. In the next section, there are online or videoconferencing services; professional therapists are affiliated there as well.

You can, of course, always start out with a referral from a family physician, friends, or relatives.

American Academy of Child and Adolescent Psychiatry (AACAP)
www.aacap.org

American Association of Pastoral Counselors (AAPC)
www.aapc.org

American Psychological Association (APA)
www.apa.org

American Psychiatric Association (APA)
www.psychiatry.org

National Association of Social Workers (NASW)
Socialworkers.org

Text, Email, Phone, or Video Conferencing

Better Help Online Therapy
www.betterhelp.com
A network of licensed psychologists, social workers, and marriage and family counselors providing online or virtual therapy for a fee.

Talkspace
Talkspace.com
Online therapy begins with a 60-second online assessment.

Online-Therapy.com
Based on CBT (cognitive behavior therapy).

Crisis text line
741741
(Although the service is free, it depends on the plane you have for your cell phone service whether there will be text messaging charges or not)

Friendship coaches, experts, and related blogs
https://www.drjanyager.com
www.whenfriendshiphurts.com
Friendship coach and author Dr. Jan Yager's websites. Sign up for her mailing list through the site. There is also a blog at drjanyager.com with articles related to friendship, time management, and Dr. yager's other areas of expertise.

Shondaland
https://www.shondaland.com
writer and producer Shonda Rhimes (her hit shows include *Grey's Anatomy* and *Station 19,* created this website which includes a regular blog entitled, 'The Art of Friendship."

Project BFF
Project-bff.com
Manya Chylinski and Terri Birkeland are co-founders. The project has a blog and podcast. Although free, you can become a patron through Patreon.

Jillian Richardson
www.thatjillian.com

Sema Rubins (UK)
Listed in Life Coach-Directory.org.uk

Shasta Nelson
Founder and CEO of GirlFriendCircles.com

Dr. Marisa G. Franco

Dr. Miriam Kirmayer
miriamkirmayer.com

Christy Pennison
Christypennison.com

Expertise Finder, Toronto, Canada
info@expertisefinder.com

Danielle Bayard
www.daniellebayardjackson.com

Irene S. Levine, Ph.D.
Irenelevine.com

The Social Skills Center
Socialskillscenter.com

Apps and Websites for Meeting New Friends
Cautionary note: Whatever app or website you are using, be careful and cautious about meeting anyone new and unfamiliar to you in person. In my book, *125 Ways to Meet the Love of Your Life,* I devote an entire chapter to staying safe during the search. Even though you're looking for a new friend, you still must play it safe if you consider meeting in person. In a nutshell:

- Find out enough about someone through e-mails, texts, phone calls, Google searches, and even background checks, before you agree to meet in person especially if you do not already have any friends in common.
- Keep the connection online and at a distance until you feel comfortable moving it off-line. Do not let anyone pressure you into meeting in-person before you are ready. Always meet for the first time in a public place with people around.
- Preferably bring another friend along with you for that initial meeting in a public place.

https://bumble.com
https://bumble.com/en-us/bff (Bumble BFF)
Founded in 2014 and headquartered in Austin, Texas, although most associate Bumble with a dating site/app, it is also being used to meet platonic friends.

www.friendship.com.au
The Friendship Page, started in 1996 by Australian Bronwyn Polson, includes a friendship

chat room, quotes on friendship, as well as highlighting the annual International Friendship Day.

www.girlfriendcircles.com
Founded by friendship author Shasta Nelson, a membership friendship networking site to help women connect locally. Nelson also organizes and leads international trips for women.

LMK
https://www.lmk.chat
This is an app that you can download from the App Store or Google Play with the tag line "make new friends."

Next door
https://nextdoor.com
An app that enables neighbors to connect with each other.

www.selfgrowth.com
Free online resources on friendship and other relationship topics.

http://whatfriendsdo.com
This site has helped thousands to better help a friend in need.

www.Facebook.com (now known as Meta)
Free site for staying connected to, and even meeting, new friends.

www.LinkedIn.com
Free international networking site for business friendships and relationships.

Meetup
https://www.meetup.com
Meetup groups bring people together with shared interests.

Hey! VINA
https://www.heyvina.com
Peanut
https://www.peanut-app.io

Skout
https://www.skout.com
Started in 2007. It's a friendship and a dating app that fosters connection with others if you find yourself traveling.

Wink
https://www.getwinkapp.com

Yubo
https://www.yubo.live/

Road Scholar

www.roadscholar.org
Adult exchange program offering organized trips.

Friendship Force International
www.friendship-force.org
Friendship Force, founded in 1977 with chapters throughout U.S. and globally. Its "citizen ambassadors" live with host families.

Information About Annual Friendship Events

Chase's Calendar of Events. Updated annual beginning in 1957. For more information, go to: https://rowman.com/page/chases

National Day Calendar
Founded in 2013.
https://www.nationaldaycalendar.com

Loneliness Resources

https://www.oprah.com/health/just-say-hello-how-to-participate
Oprah Winfrey has partnered with Skype in a campaign to reduce loneliness.

Project UNLonely
https://www.artandhealing.org
The Foundation for Art and Healing launched its campaign to combat loneliness in 2016.

Campaign to End Loneliness
https://www.campaigntoendloneliness.org
The Campaign to End Loneliness is legally part of the What Works Centre for Wellbeing, headquartered in London, England.

Volunteering

Chapter 30 in my book, *Help Yourself Now: A Practical Guide to Finding the Information and Assistance You Need* (Allworth Press, 2021) is devoted to Volunteerism. As I write in the introduction to the annotated listings in that chapter, "You [and your friend or group of friends] could volunteer related to a cause that you care about, such as a health-related issue, where an organization has paid staff but relies on volunteers to augment what they do, especially for fund=raising walks or runs or galas and the related silent or charity auctions. Or you could volunteer related to an interest or hobby that you [and your friend or friends} have."

AARP
https://createthegood.aarp.org
There is a lot of information at the AARP site about volunteering together with friends.

Helping Abroad
https://www.helpingabroad.org
Since 1998, this organization has been helping to match up volunteers with programs. Although not a free volunteer program, it keeps the weekly fee to volunteers as affordable as possible.

Together We Can Change the World (TWCCTW)
http://twcctw.org
Two friends, speaker/singer Jana Stanfield and speaker/author Scott Friedman, started this volunteer initiative back in 2008. Several times a year, they work on projects in South East Asia to help disadvantaged children, especially orphans, and women to improve their day-to-day lives as well as their educational chances.

Volunteer Forever
www.volunteerforever.com

International Volunteer HQ
https://www.volunteerhq.org

Works Cited and Further References

AARP. "Fun with Friends: Make Volunteering a Group Effort." Posted at https://createthegood.aarp.org

ABC Movie of the Week. "Brian's Song." Written by William Blinn. First aired November 30, 1971. Starring James Caan and Billy Dee Williams.

Adamczyk, Amy. "On Thanksgiving and Collective Memory: Constructing the American Tradition." *Journal of Historical Sociology*, September 3, 2022, Volume 15, Number 3, pages 343-365.

Afshar, Melissa Fleur. "Woman Wanting Gift Back After Wedding Called Off Divides Internet: 'Cringe'" Posted on *Newsweek* online, November 20, 2023.

Albom, Mitch. *Tuesdays with Morrie.* NY: Crown, 2002 (1997).

Allen, Jennie. Find Your People: *Building Deep Community in a Lonely World.* WaterBrook, 2022.

Alonso, Johanna. "The New Plague on Campus: Loneliness." November 8, 2023. Posted online at insidehighered.com.

Anh, Nguyen Nhat. *I See Yellow Flowers in the Green Grass.* Stamford, CT: Hannacroix Creek Books, Inc., 2021.

Aniftos, Rania. "Sweetest Friendship Bracelet Moments at Taylor Swift's Eras Tour." August 11, 2023. Posted at Billboard.com

Aristotle. The Nicomachean Ethics. Translated with an Introduction by David Ross. Revised by J.L. Ackrill and J.O. Urmson. NY: Oxford University Press, 1998. (Book VIII and IX: Friendship)

Asmelash, Leah. "How Friendsgiving Found Its Place in the Holiday Season." Posted online at CNN, November 21, 2021.

Associated Press, "Taylor Swift's The Eros Tour Becomes the first to Gross #1bn—report." Published in *The Guardian* online, December 8, 2023.

Attri, Dr. Raman K. *Speed Matters: Why Best in Class Business Leaders Prioritize Workforce Time to Proficiency Metrics.* Speed to Proficiency Research, 2021.

Blau, Peter M. *Exchange and Power in Social Life.* New York: Wiley, 1964.

Bonesteel, Matt. "Gale Sayer's Speech in 'Brian's Song' is an Essential Piece of Sports-movie History." September 23, 2020. Posted online at washingtonpost.com

Brandt, Jenn and Callie Clare. *An Introduction to Popular Culture in the US: People, Politics, and Power.* NY: Bloomsbury Academic, 2018.

Brashares, Ann. *Sisterhood of the Traveling Pants.* NY: Delacorte, 2001.

Callanan, Maggie and Patricia Kelley. *Final Gifts.* NY: Ballantine Books, 1993.

Carnegie, Dale. *How to Win Friends and Influence People.* NY: Pocket Books, 1998, 1936.

CBS News Sunday Morning. "The Power of Friendships." November 2, 2003, posted at cbsnews.com/stories.

Chamberlain, Ben. SNAP-Ed/EFNEP State Coordinator. "The right size for Any Party." - February 14, 2012. Posted online by Michigan State University, MSU Extension.

Chase's Calendar of Events. Updated annual beginning in 1957. For more information, go to: https://rowman.com/page/chases

Classamtes.com "Classmates.com Celebrates National New Friends, Old Friends Week." May 2, 2006, press release, John Uppendahl, Vice President of Public Relations & Community Affairs, Renton, Washington.

Colarossi, L. and Eccles J. "differential Effects of Support Providers on Adolescent Mental Health." *Social Work Research.*, 2003, Volume 27, pages 19-30.

Corbin, Ian and Joe Water. "What the Surgeon General Missed About America's Loneliness Epidemic." Opinion. *Newsweek.* Posted online May 16, 2023.

Dagan, Yael and Joel Yager. "Addressing Loneliness in Complex PTSD." *Journal of Nervous & Mental Disease.* Volume 207. 2019, pages 433-439.

Dart, Iris R. *Beaches.* NY: William Morrow, 2004 (1985).

Dunbar, Robin. *Friends: Understanding our Most Important Relationships.* NY: Little Brown, 2022.

Emerson, Ralph Waldo. *Essays by Ralph Waldo Emerson.* Introduction by Irwin Edman. NY: Harper & Row, 1951 (1926). See First Series, "Friendship."

Emmrich, Stuart. _In the Annals of Party Throwing, Stephen Schwarzman Has Some Competition." Posted at *The New York Times* website, February 15, 2017.

Fisher, Ray and Dave Koco. *Lucky the Orphan.* Stamford, CT: Hannacroix Creek Books, Inc., 2021.

Flora, Carlin. "Awkward Encounters." *Psychology Today,* May/June 2009, pages 88-93.

Franco, Marisa G. Platonic: *How the Science of Attachment Can Help You Make—and Keep--Your Friends.* NY: Putnam's, 2022.

Freeman, Lucy. *Fight Against Fears.* NY: Praeger, 1982 (1951).

Friedrichs, David O. *Law in Our Lives: An Introduction.* NY: Oxford University Press, 2011.

Gibran, Kahlil. *The Prophet.* London: Heinemann, 1969. (First published 1926)

Giles, Lynne, G. Glonek, M. Luszcz, and G. Andrews. "Effect of Social Networks on 10-year Survival in Very Old Australians: The Australian Longitudinal Study of Aging." Journal of Epidemiology & Community Health. July 2005, Volume 59, pages 574-579.

Goodreads." "Franklin D. Roosevelt Quotes." Posted at https://www.goodreads.com/quotes/1542488-do-something-if-it-works-do-more-of-it-if

Hartup, W.W. "The Company They Keep: Friendships and Their Developmental Significant." *Child Development*, 1996, pages 1-13Hay, Louise. L. *Power Thoughts: 365 Daily Affirmations.* Carlsbad, CA: Hay House, 1999.

Holden, Stan. *Growing Your Business Can be as Fun & Easy as... Giving Candy to Strangers.* Woodway, TX: Natane Press, 2015.

Homans, Georg. "Social Behavior as Exchange." *The American Journal of Sociology.* 1958. Volume 63, pages 597-606.

Horton, Tom. "Seeing Friends Regularly Lowers Dementia Risk, Study Suggests" Posted online at the Independent (UK), August 3, 2019.

Hughes, Mary Elizabeth, Linda J. Waite, Louise C. Hawkley, and John T. Cacioppo. "a short Scale for Measuring Loneliness in Large Surveys." *Research on Aging,* November 2004, Volume 26, pages 655-672.

Huston, Ted L. and Rodney M. Cate. "Social Exchange in Intimate Relationships." Part of *Love and Attraction,* edited by M. Cook and G. Wilson. Oxford: Pergamon Press, 1979.

Hutchinson, Susan L., Careen M. Yarnal, Julie Staffordson, and Deborah L. Kerstetter. "Beyond Fun and Friendship: The Red Hat Society as a Coping Resource for Older Women." *Aging & Society,* 2008, pages 978-999.

Kelly, Samantha Murphy. "How the Taylor Swift and Travis Kelce Connection Started with a Friendship Bracelet." Posted online at CNN Business, September 25, 2023.

Komter, Aafke and Wilma Vollebergh. "Gift Giving and the Emotional Significance of Family and Friends." *Journal of Marriage and the Family.* August 1997, Volume 59, pages 747-757.

Lalli, Judy. *I Like Being Me: Poems About Kindness, Friendship, and Making Good Choices.* Minneapolis, MN: Free Spirit Publishers, 2017.

Levin, Gail. *Hopper's Places.* NY: Alfred A. Knopf, 1986. (Reprinted by University of California Press, 1998)

Lough, Loree. *From Ashes to Honor.* Nashville, TN: Abington Press, 2011.

Maltz, Maxwell. *Psycho-Cybernetics*. NY: Pocket Books, 1969 (1960).

Manchanda, Tanya, Alan Stein, and Mina Fazel. "Investigating the Role of Friendship Interventions on the Mental Health Outcomes of Adolescents: A Scoping Review of Range and a Systematic Review of Effectiveness." *International Journal of Environmental Research and Public Health*. January 25, 2023.

McDonald, Kerry. "Harvard Study: An Epidemic of Loneliness Is Spreading Across America." Posted February 19, 2021, Making Caring Common Project, Harvard University Graduate School of Education.

McGuinness, Alan Loy. *The Friendship Factor*. Minneapolis, MN: Augsburg Fortress Publishers, 1979.
Mikhail, Alexa. "Loneliness is a Health Crisis Comparable to Smoking Up to 15 Cigarettes a Day." Posted at Fortune.com on June 15, 2023.

Miles, Josephin, editor. *Classic Essays in English.* Second edition. Boston: Little, Brown and Company, 1965. (Includes "Of Friendship" by Sir Francis Bacon.

Mills, C. Wright. *The Sociological Imagination*. NY: Oxford University Press, 2000. (Originally published in 1959)

Montaigne. *The Complete Essays of Montaigne*. Translated by Donald M. Frame. Redwood City, CA; Stanford University Press, 1958.

Murstein, Bernard L., Mary Cerreto, and Marcia G. Macdonald. "a theory and Investigation of the Effect of Exchange Orientation on Marriage and Friendship." *Journal of Marriage and the Family.* August 1977. Page 543-548.

National Day Calendar. Printed annually. (www.nationaldaycalendar.com)

National Institute on Aging (NIA). Frequent social contact in midlife may reduce dementia risk, Whitehall II study analysis shows." October 28, 2019. (Research highlights)

Nelson, Shasta. *Friendships Don'ts Just Happen.* Nashville, TN: Turner, 2013.

_____. *Frientimacy.* NY: Seal Press, 2016.Newman, Mildred and Bernard Berkowitz, with Jean Owen, *How to Be Your Own Best Friend.* NY: Random House, 1971.

Pilon, Kate. "How to Volunteer Abroad with a Friend." Posted online at International Volunteer HQ. n.d.

Putnam, Robert D. *Bowling Alone*. Revised edition. NY: Simon & Schuster, 2020. (2000)

Roden, Bex. "5 Famous Literary Quotes Explained: "'Tis Better to have loved and lost than never to have loved at all" Posted online at historythroughfiction.com, August 24, 2023.

Schwartz, Barry. "The Social Psychology of the Gift." *The American Journal of Sociology,* July 1967, Volume 73, pages 1-11.

Sommerlad A, et al. "Association of social contact with dementia and cognition: 28-year follow-up of the Whitehall II cohort study." *PLOS Medicine*. 2019;16(8): e1002862.

Trestrail, Joanne. "Studying the Roots and Reasons for Traditional Celebration." Posted at the *Chicago Tribune* website, chicagotribune.com, October 8, 2000.

Union Square & Co. *Poems on Friendship*. Signature Select Classics. NY: Union Square & Co, 2022.

Weiss, Robert. *Loneliness*. Cambridge, MA: MIT Press, 1975.

Weissbourd, Richard, Milena Batanova, Virginia Levison, and Eric. Torres. "Loneliness in America," Harvard Graduate School of Education, Making Caring Common, 13-page report.

Welty, Eudora and Ronald A. Sharp, editors. *The Norton Anthology of Friendship*. NY: 1991.

Yager, Fred and Jan Yager. *Just Your Everyday People*. Stamford, CT: Hannacroix Creek Books, Inc., 2004.

_____. *Untimely Death*. Stamford, CT: Hannacroix Creek Books, Inc., 1998.

Yager, Jan. *365 Daily Affirmations for Friendship*. Stamford, CT: Hannacroix Creek, 2012.

_____.*365 Daily Affirmations for Healthy & Nurturing Relationships*. Audiobook narrated by Lindsay Arber. Stamford, CT: Hannacroix Creek Books, Inc., 2016.

_____. "Copy of New Audience Survey (Friendship). SurveyMonkey. Snowball sample, Distributed 10/16/2023 to 11/28, 2023 (37 respondents).

_____. *Friendgevity: Making and Keeping the Friends Who Enhance and Even Extend Your Life*. Stamford, CT: Hannacroix Creek Books, Inc., 1999, 1997.

_____. *Friendshifts: The Power of Friendship and How It Shapes Our Lives. 2nd edition*. Stamford, CT: Hannacroix Creek Books, Inc., 1999, 1997.

_____. *Help Yourself Now*. NY: Allworth Press, 2021.

_____. New Audience Survey (Friendship). SurveyMonkey, October 11, 2023.

_____. *Productive Relationships*. Stamford, CT: Hannacroix Creek Books, 2011.

_____. *Putting WHEN FRIENDSHIP HURTS to Work: Exercises and Activities to Deal with Friends Who Betray, Abandon, or Wound You, Plus Help in Finding and Keeping Good Friends*. Stamford, CT: Hannacroix Creek Books, 2024.

_____. "Ten Friends That Every Woman Needs." Published in *Cosmopolitan, Marie Claire, Cosmo Girl*. 2005.

_____. "Tips for Holiday Cards, Executive Gifts and Seasonal Entertaining." *Westchester County Business Journal*, November 21, 1994, page 26.

_____. *When Friendship Hurts: How to Deal with Friends Who Betray, Abandon, or Wound You.* Second edition. New York: Simon & Schuster, Touchstone, 2024, 2002.

_____. *Who's That Sitting at My Desk? Friendship, Workshop, or Foe?* Stamford, CT: Hannacroix Creek Books, Inc., 2004.

Yager, Jeff. *Chuck & Alfonzo.* Illustrated children's book with artwork by Nancy Batra. Stamford, CT: Hannacroix Creek Books, inc., 2016. Paperback version, 2023.

_____, *Seven Days in Virtual Reality* (A Novel) Stamford, CT: Hannacroix Creek Books, 2021.

Zaraska, Marta. *Growing Young: How Friendship, Optimism, and Kindness Can Help You Live to 100.* NY: Random House, 2020.

Contact Information for Friends

Name _____

e-mail address _____

Cell phone/texts _____

Address_____

_____

_____

Notes? _____

_____

Entered/Updated _____

Name _____

e-mail address _____

Cell phone/texts _____

Address_____

_____

_____

Notes? _____

_____

Entered/Updated _____

Name _____

e-mail address _____

Cell phone/texts _____

Address_____

_____

_____

Notes? _____

_____

Entered/Updated _____

Name _____

e-mail address _____

Cell phone/texts _____

Address_____

_____

_____

Notes? _____

_____

Entered/Updated _____

Contact Information for Friends

Name _____

e-mail address _____

Cell phone/texts _____

Address_____

_____

_____

Notes? _____

_____

Entered/Updated _____

Name _____

e-mail address _____

Cell phone/texts _____

Address_____

_____

_____

Notes? _____

_____

Entered/Updated _____

Name _____

e-mail address _____

Cell phone/texts _____

Address_____

_____

_____

Notes? _____

_____

Entered/Updated _____

Name _____

e-mail address _____

Cell phone/texts _____

Address_____

_____

_____

Notes? _____

_____

Entered/Updated _____

Record for Cards, Gifts, and Events

Date	Friend	Card	Gift	Event

Record for Cards, Gifts, and Events
RECEIVED FROM OTHERS (OR SHARED)

Date	Friend	Card	Gift	Event

Friendship Photos

Notes

Notes

About the Author

Jan Yager, Ph.D., a friendship coach, sociologist, speaker, and author of such bestselling books on friendship including *When Friendship Hurts* (Simon & Schuster), translated into 29 languages, *Friendshifts: The Power of Friendship and How It Shapes Our Lives*, which led to appearances on *Oprah, The View, the Today Show, CBS Sunday Morning; 365 Daily Affirmations for Friendship; Friendship Thoughts, Famous Quotes, and a Journal,* and, most recently, *Putting WHEN FRINDSHIP HURTS to Work: Exercises and Activities to Deal with Friends Who Betray, Abandon, or Wound You, Plus Help in Finding and Keeping Good Friends..*

Jan has an MA in Criminal Justice and a Ph.D. in Sociology (CUNY Graduate Center). She also did a year of graduate work in art therapy at Hahnemann Medical College. Her BA is in Fine Arts from Hofstra University. She has had two one-person art shows of her artwork.

Jan has given talks, or conducted workshops, throughout the U.S. and globally on friendship and on her other areas of expertise: work relationships, time management, crime victims, and writing and getting published.

For more on this prolific author, go to her main website: https://www.drjanyager.com

Selected Related Books by the Author

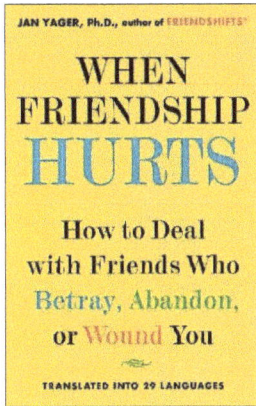

When Friendship Hurts
How to Deal with Friends who Betray, Abandon, or Wound You
Second edition
Simon & Schuster, 2024, 2002
(Available in e-book, print, and audiobook versions)
We've all had friendships that have gone bad. Whether it takes the form of a simple yet inexplicable estrangement or a devastating betrayal, a failed friendship can make your life miserable, threaten your success at work or school, and even undermine your romantic relationships. Finally, there is help. *When Friendship Hurts* explores what causes friendships to falter and explains how to mend them – or end them. In this straightforward, illuminating book filled with dozens of quizzes and real-life examples.

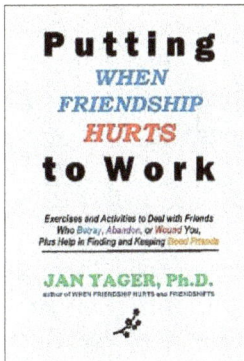

Putting WHEN FRIENDSHIP HURTS to Work
A unique, practical workbook that is a companion to *When Friendship Hurts* or it could be used as a standalone workbook. Filled with exercises and activities with a place to write in your answers. Illustrated with color photographs and line drawings throughout. In the back is a Resource section with associations, apps, websites, and even friendship coaches for follow-up.
After a brief Author's Note and Introduction, there are nine chapters with activities and exercises to be completed related to the theme of that chapter such as "can This Friendship Be Saved?" or "When and How to End It."

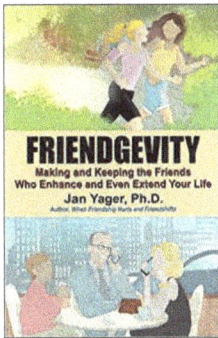

Friendgevity
Making and Keeping the Friends who Enhance and Even Extend Your Life
Available in e-book, print, and audiobook formats.
This prescriptive self-help book explores how the right friends can extend your life, delay, or avoid the onset of dementia, help with recovery from heart disease, cancer, and other illnesses, and better withstand pain. However, the wrong ones – frenemies and fatal friends – can have catastrophic effects. Appendix IV is "Applying the Four Sociological Theories to Friendship" and Appendix VII is "Critical Thinking Questions." There is also a reading Group Guide for students or Book Club members.

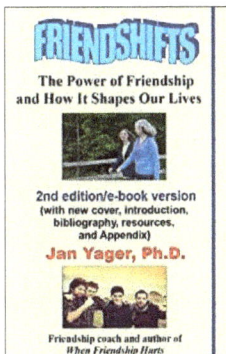

Friendshifts
The Power of Friendship and How It Shapes Our Lives
Available in e-book, print, and audiobook formats.
"Rewarding, sensible self-help manual for making, keeping, and improving friendships.... sociologist Yager's how-to takes its title from a word she coined, which refers to the way friendships change as we move through life's stages...." — *Publishers Weekly*
"...provides a new way for you to look at, and understand, friendship so you can be a better friend (and have more satisfying friendships).
—   From "Oprah's Books — Books Seen on the Show, "Have You Forgotten Your Friends?" (10/28/99)

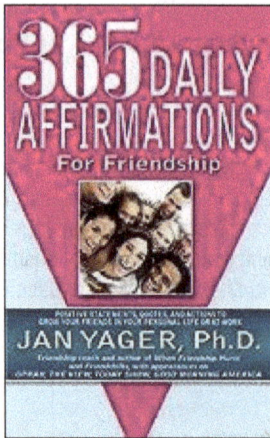

365 Daily Affirmations for Friendship

Available in e-book, print, and audiobook formats.
In addition to the 365 friendship affirmations, as well as activities to improve friendship in your personal life and at work, there is an introduction about friendship.
Sampler affirmations:

1.   "I am worthy of a positive friendship."
26.   : I remember my friends' birthdays."
149. : I cheer myself on as well as my friends through the tough and the joyful times."

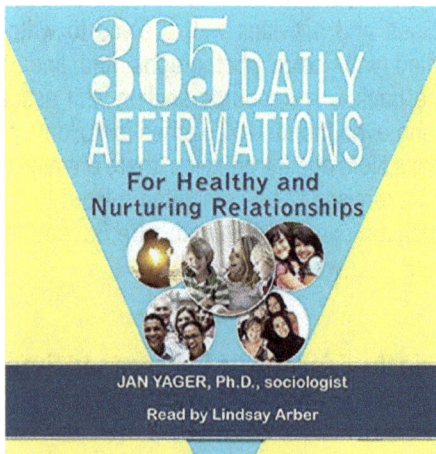

365 Daily Affirmations for Healthy & Nurturing Relationships

Available in e-book, print, and audiobook formats.
(Narrated by actress Lindsay Arber)
Positive statements related to key relationships including parent-child, sibling, extended family, friend, romantic partner, neighbors, co-workers, or service providers. Includes an Introduction by Dr. Jan Yager as well as activities.

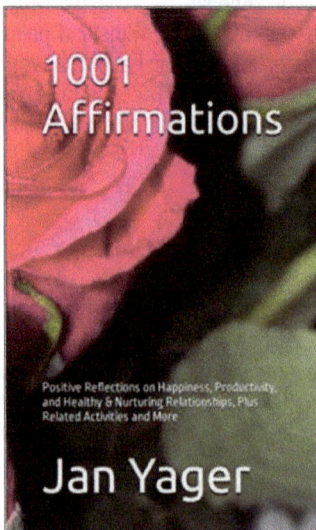

1 Affirmations

Available in e-book and paperback print. This book combines 3 affirmations books: *365 Daily Affirmations for Happiness, 365 Daily Affirmations for Time Management,* and *365 Daily Affirmations for Healthy & Nurturing Relationships.*

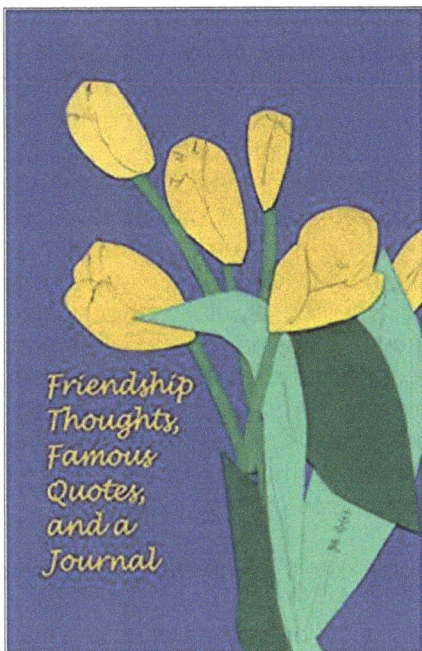

Friendship Thoughts, Famous Quotes, and a Journal
176 pages
Available in trade paperback or hardcover
A unique friendship journal including an Introduction by friendship expert Jan Yager, Ph.D., followed by 140 quotes on friendship written by philosophers, essayists, poets, playwrights, celebrities, psychologists, sociologists, authors, and leaders that the author has been gathering for decades.

Each quote is reprinted at the top of a blank lined page where you can journal. After the quotes/lined blank pages, there are four additional pages for your own or other friendship quotes plus two blank pages for drawings or photos.

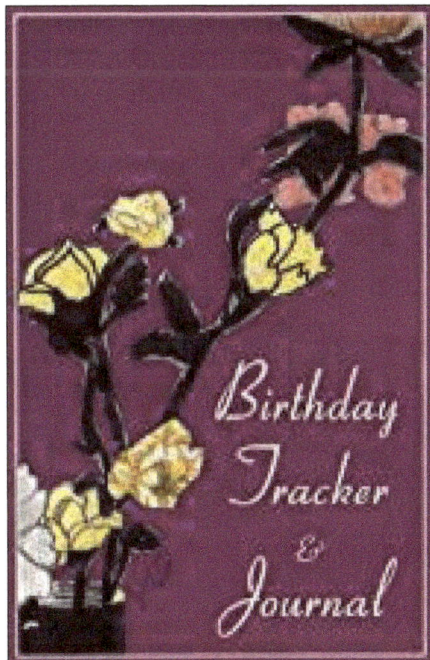

Birthday Tracker & Journal
Available in print- paperback and hardcover.
Provides a special place to record important birthdays for family, friends, and others, month by month. It includes an informative Introduction to birthday celebration traditions, and lists birthday birthstones and flowers by month for gift-giving considerations. Color illustrations by author/artist Dr. Jan Yager appear throughout.

You (or your friends) will never forget a birthday again!

WHO'S THAT SITTING AT MY DESK?

How to succeed by mastering work relationships

Jan Yager

"This book shows you how to work well with others to supercharge your career."
–Brian Tracy, best-selling author and speaker

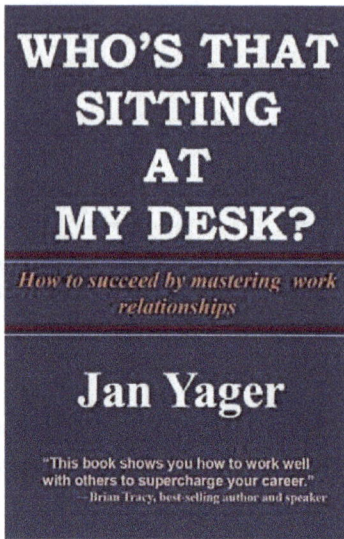

Who's That Sitting at My Desk?
Workship, Friendship, or Foe?
Available in e-book print, and audiobook versions
Building on decades of research into workplace issues and friendship patterns, sociologist and consultant Dr. Jan Yager offers insights into how to succeed by mastering workplace relationships. Based on an international survey of 400 men and women and over 100 interviews, Yager discovered a relationship unique to the workplace and business. She calls it a *workship*--more connected than an acquaintance but not as intimate or as potentially complicated as a as a friend. *Workships*, especially positive ones, help work to be more productive and more fun. Work friendships are also explored.

Yager is the author of *Business Protocol, When Friendship Hurts, Friendshifts,* and *Friendgevity,* among other titles.
Praise: "*Who's That Sitting at My Desk?* is the best researched and most useful book on getting along with friends and foes at work that I've ever read. Don't go to work without it!" -Don Gabor

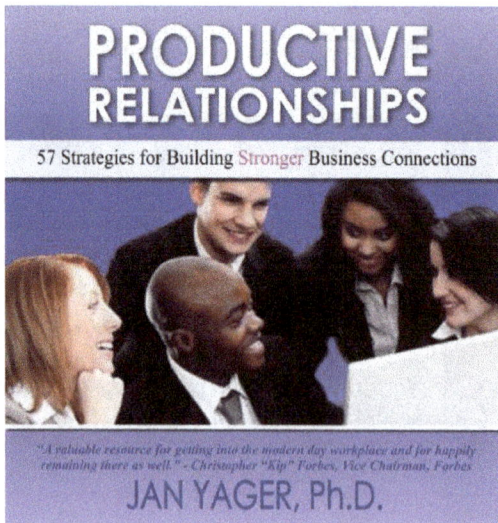

PRODUCTIVE RELATIONSHIPS

57 Strategies for Building Stronger Business Connections

"*A valuable resource for getting into the modern day workplace and for happily remaining there as well.*" - Christopher "Kip" Forbes, Vice Chairman, Forbes

JAN YAGER, Ph.D.

Productive Relationships
57 Strategies for Building Stronger Business Connections
Audiobook narrated by Stephanie Murphy
(Also available in e-book, paperback and hardcover print editions)
A practical guide to developing productive business relationships to hasten your success, whether you work for a major corporation, a small business, or are a self-employed entrepreneur or freelancer.
Includes a discussion about work friendships.

Jan Yager, Ph.D., whose bosses, over the years, have included legendary publisher Barney Rosset, Pulitzer Prize-winning author Norman Mailer, and academic chairs, did extensive original interviews and observations for this useful book that covers everything from how to recognize and deal with negative types you might encounter at work and in business to more effective use of social media.

Looking Backward, Going Forward: Reflections on a Writer's Life

Illustrated with color photographs throughout
Available in e-book, print, and audiobook formats

In addition to sharing about her career, Jan shares about her personal life including her first marriage, which started off in a tragic way, a week after her brother was murdered in a robbery/homicide. That marriage ended after three years but thirteen years later, as you will read about in this memoir, she put two ads in *New York* magazine when she was a successful, 35-year-old Assistant Professor at a college on Long Island. Everyone thought she had it all and couldn't understand why Jan even wanted to get married again. But Jan wanted to share her life with that special someone and to have a family. Her second ad was successful and, as you will read in her memoir, 23 days after they met, Jan and Fred surprised everyone by getting married and going on to have a happy marriage including raising their two sons, Scott and Jeffrey, now grown and with families of their own.

Jan's memoir discusses her friends over the years, but it also goes beyond sharing about her life by including insights into her key areas of expertise – friendship, crime victims; time management; writing and getting published.

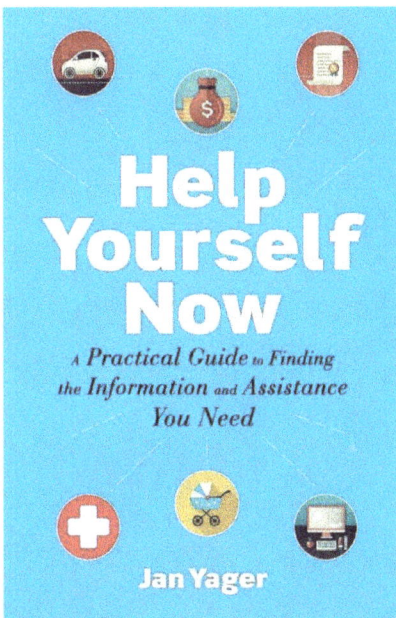

Help Yourself Now

A Practical Guide to Finding the Information and Assistance You Need

Allworth Press, 2021

Available in e-book and paperback print editions

There are 31 chapters covering everything from Addiction, Adoption and Foster Care, Aging, Arts, Children and teens, Crime Victims, witnesses, and Prevention to Health and Wellness, Legal Services, pregnancy and childbearing to Veterans and Volunteerism. Each chapter has an overview followed by annotated listings of where to get help.

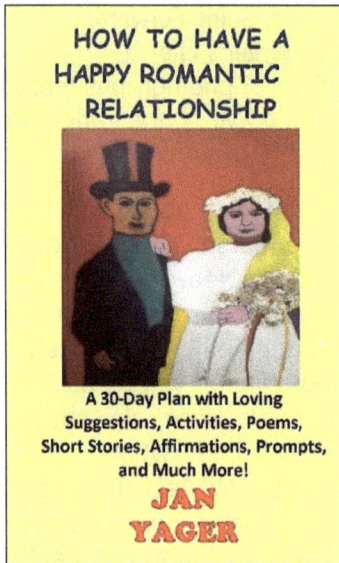

How to Have a Happy Romantic Relationship

A 30-Day Plan with Loving Suggestions, Activities, Poems, Short Stories, Affirmations, Prompts, and Much More!

2026

Celebrating Friends and Friendship concentrates on our friends. This prescriptive, self-help book provides practical insights and tips for couples who want love that lasts *and* works.

It is written by sociologist Jan Yager, Ph.D. who draws on decades of research, coaching, and teaching related college courses, as well as her own happy 41-year marriage to Fred Yager. *How to Have a Happy Romantic Relationship* explores what helps romantic relationships thrive over time: communication that connects, independence that strengthens rather than threatens love, and shared experiences that build resilience when life gets complicated. You'll find playlists of songs to listen or dance to, month-by-month activity suggestions, prompts to speak or write your answers to, an extensive resource section, poems, two short stories, and lots more. Color photographs and artwork reproductions throughout.

Around the World in 80 Ways

AROUND THE WORLD IN 80 WAYS

Make Your Travel Dreams Come True No Matter How Much Time or Money You Have to Spend

2024

This unique book shows how international travel can be life-changing, relationship-strengthening, and surprisingly affordable. With vivid color photographs throughout, this book offers 60 ways you can get paid to pay to travel and 20 additional ways you can pay for them, proving that money doesn't have to be the reason friends put their dreams on hold. All 80 ways to travel should pay you back emotionally and experientially.

Travel with one of your friends or a group of friends. Celebrate your friend's birthday in Iceland, go with a friend to a writing retreat in Scotland, or plan a high school reunion that combines cooking and friendship in Tuscany.

Jan's Selected Fiction

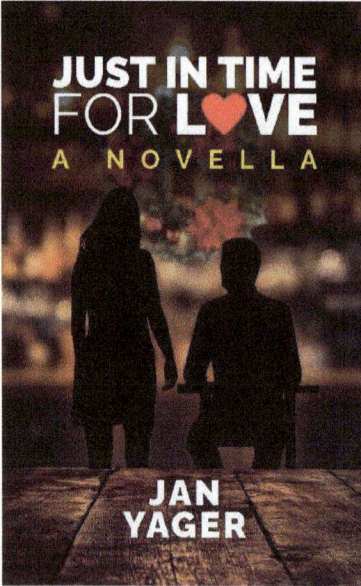

Just in Time for Love

A Novella

2026

Available in e-book and print formats

Kate Hellman has built a successful life helping others get organized, and as an assistant college professor, but when it comes to love, she's always running a little late. Joe Wexler, a creative entrepreneur nursing a broken heart, isn't looking for romance—until one unexpected meeting changes both of their plans.

As Kate and Joe navigate attraction, uncertainty, and timing, each lean on a best friend who offers perspective, humor, and much-needed honesty. In *Just in Time for Love*, friendship matters as much as romance—because sometimes it's our friends who help us take the biggest emotional risks.

Warm, witty, and hopeful, this contemporary novella explores connection, second chances, and why love—though complicated—is worth the risk.

Just in Time for Love: A Novella is based on the original screenplay titled "No Time for Love" by Fred Yager and Jan Yager.

www.ingramcontent.com/pod-product-compliance
Lightning Source LLC
Chambersburg PA
CBHW081419270326
41931CB00015B/3337